Dispossessed Daughters of Eve

Dispossessed Daughters of Eve

Faith and Feminism

New Edition

SUSAN DOWELL
AND
LINDA HURCOMBE

First published in Great Britain 1981 by SCM Press Ltd

This revised edition published 1987 by
SPCK
Holy Trinity Church
Marylebone Road
London NW1 4DU

British Library Cataloguing in Publication Data

Dowell, Susan
    Dispossessed daughters of Eve : faith and
    feminism.—New ed.
    1. Women in Christianity 2. Women—
    Social conditions
    I. Title II. Hurcombe, Linda
    261.8'3442   HQ1394

    ISBN 0–281–04292–6

    Phototypeset by Input Typesetting Ltd
    Printed in Great Britain by
    Dotesios Printers Ltd, Bradford-on-Avon

Contents

The quotation from T. S. Eliot's *Ash Wednesday* on p. 55 is used by kind permission of Faber & Faber; from Robin Morgan's poem 'The City of God' from her book *Lady of the Beasts* on p. 55 by kind permission of Random House Inc; and from Adrienne Rich, *On Lies, Secrets and Silences* on p. 112 by kind permission of Virago.

Preface

Our collaboration on this book actually began in the early days of our friendship, when we began to discern common threads of concern in both our lives. These ties and connections sprang up and grew naturally: both of us had been involved in the peace movement since university days; both of us were Christian, but profoundly dissatisfied as our growing consciousness of sexual apartheid in the church gained clarity; both of us were married to clergymen and had young children; and we shared the ubiquitous dilemmas of clergy wives everywhere.

We began more and more to consult each other about our lives, to seek support from each other. 'Hey Linda, what do you think about the letter that bishop's wife wrote about vicar's wives making nonsense of "women's lib"?' 'I think she's wrong.' 'Me too. Shall we write a letter to the editor?' The writing collaboration grew, with more letters, poems to accompany liturgical dance, sermons, lectures, book reviews. More and more, the focus of our mutual energies was the 'woman' question. In the devastating let-down after General Synod's vote against women's ordination in November 1978 (see chapter 5) we turned to each other when even our dearest male comrades could not fully fathom our sense of rejection. It was probably this experience more than any single other that forced our feminism, somehow previously compartmentalized and at distance from church and liturgy, to emerge and to connect with theological perspectives and form a critique of the deep-seated illness we perceived in the church.

We come from very different backgrounds. Linda was made in America; much of her childhood was steeped in Bible belt fundamentalism. The greatest legacy of this background is that the Bible in all its heights and depths is well-trodden terrain. Her Church of Christ college in the South, jokingly referred to as 'East Jesus State', prided itself in ensuring that every student remaining in its hallowed halls long enough to graduate would leave with a 'major' in biblical studies. (It also promised without apology to find suitable husbands for its women students: after all, wasn't that why they'd come?) Susan was educated at a Church of England school, frequently truanted from Sunday school, and grew into a healthy atheistic certainty in secondary school. At university, she rejoined the church, moved by the commitment of Christian friends and teachers to movements for liberation, peace and equality. She had some difficulty convincing Linda that an intimate knowledge of the Bible could not be presupposed among Anglicans in this country. Part of her preparation for the book was a careful reading of the Bible.

Our two very different childhood traditions have taught us that the church holds and guards some special truths about women's nature and their place in God's creation. We have put this claim to the test and have been compelled in all honesty to shed the 'special truths' argument as the church presently interprets it. We remain nevertheless committed to the church and maintain a conviction that Christian feminism has something important to teach the community whose name is 'church'. This book is an attempt to clarify the crisis which, ignored or not, undoubtedly exists.

The letters which informed the book in its early stages were an important test of the accuracy of our observations. Was the anger we had come to feel about the direction of the church regarding women as widespread nationally as we assumed? We advertised in a national newspaper and in several women's publications. We were deluged with replies. We then researched further responses for a series of lectures on women and religion, and went to see our bishop to share our thoughts and fears.

The above observations formed the brief and shaped the direction of the book. In chapter 1 we present a historical and theological background to modern feminist consciousness, and challenge the lack of dialogue between the church and secular feminism. We envisage our dialogue addressing people who are at present hardly on speaking terms, but who could teach one another a good deal.

Chapter 2 is a Bible study providing a woman's view of this amazing book and acknowledges the lack of full-grown female consciousness therein, 'whatabouteries' notwithstanding. (A 'whataboutery' is our term for questions like 'What about Jael? Judith? Deborah? Huldah? – you get the drift.) The importance of understanding the Bible takes on fresh urgency in a decade commencing uneasily with the election in America of a Born Again movie cow-boy. The cults instrumental in that election are ominously wed to right-wing politics, isolationism and violence. In Britain, the cosmetically acceptable face of womanhood, our Prime Minister, mouthed in May 1979 the prayer of St Francis to gild the unacceptable face of Protestant Ethics economics. Reader, know your Bible!

Chapter 3 asks whether today's sexual dilemmas are enlightened, resolved or deepened by feminist assertion. Can the invective of the women's movement help to heal the dualistic split of spirit and flesh which has perpetuated body hatred? Can we be restored to the Hebrew and early Christian certainty that body, mind and spirit are indivisible? That our mortal flesh is indeed the temple of the Holy Spirit? We think yes. But we also come clean in this chapter about our personal unease with some of the more dominant/newsworthy dogmas of radical feminism. We confront two major contemporary issues: homosexuality and abortion.

Chapter 4 is an introduction to feminist theology. An impressive and growing body of scholarship – biblical, historical, prophetic – is crossing the Atlantic, publishers permitting, adding its weight to the work being done in this country. We recognize the need to 'do' theology for ourselves, no easy task when the church treats its female critics like rebellious daughters in a family where a major disagreement is settled by a cautious father in what he imagines to be a prudent way conducive to peace and a quiet life. While not yet widely circulated, feminist theology is gaining momentum and confidence, steadily bringing women's issues well to the fore of mainstream theological exploration.

In chapter 5 we describe the schizophrenia involved in participating in an established church which is somehow expected to hallow our national life. We draw heavily here on the letters we received and hone in on the flavour of personally experienced parochial life, including its relationship to the symbol of priesthood (as well as the significance of the substantial and successful resistance to women's ordination). The question of female priesthood is discussed specifically in this chapter, but it is also a touchstone throughout the book. More important to us has been the experience of painting our own portraits, sounding out our experiences as women against the awesome and ancient portraits handed us by the church: those traditional views which were dusted off, rehung and reapproved in the 1978 Synod 'Retrospective Exhibition'. Priestcraft, clericalism, are sinister words with a sinister history. While acknowledging its human, often lovable, occasionally saintly and now vulnerable face, we nevertheless ask how the phenomenon of clericalism relates to the undoubted quiescence of traditional church women. Our pre-eminent assertion in this chapter is that clericalism and sexism are inextricably linked.

Where better to test this theory than by looking at the role and stereotype of the vicar's wife, Daughter of the Reformation and subject of chapter 6? Undoubtedly her appearance as the wife of the priest was instrumental in restoring marriage to a degree of spiritual dignity. Her story is a kind of playing over the melody of clerical history in minor key; she who, meek, godly, and ever so practical, is wed to the trivial round, the common task, and who bears a goodly portion of the burden accompanying a defective Reformation theology of woman. The clergy marriage continues to contain many of the more traditional expectations of male/female partnership, and is thus a good place to begin an enquiry into 'old' values – to discover which are of the Kingdom of Heaven and which of the Kingdom of Big Daddy.

In chapter 7 we discuss the connection between women's absence from the formal processes of history making and the prospect of global annihilation. We accept that this absence has been crucially important in causing the imbalance which has brought us to a tragic and terrifying brink. Demands for a 'new deal' from men mark only a primitive beginning of the women's movement, and feminist vision encompasses nothing less than the hope that there is still time for a new covenant with the earth and with the whole human family. We ask what irreplaceable resources exist at the heart of the Christian gospel to incarnate hope in this fragile age.

We consciously resist the temptation to more traditional scholarship. We see this book rediscovering what the important questions are, making them palpable so as to begin acting upon them. Our eccentric methodology has taken us from lectern to library, from primary research to private letters. We offer our thought, our own version of the crisis. Above all this book is a dialogue. It has burned its way into being after many years of thought, campaigning, lecturing, and above all, through womanly trust. It has not emerged from leisured contemplation: we are not academics but we have done our homework. We did manage to carve out for ourselves two precious and fruitful retreats to the country away from phones and mundane domestic demands, and these times shine like a diamond for us. We trust that this book will resonate with your thoughts.

The letters we received were of inestimable help as we wrote the book. We thank all who responded to our advertisements, and the following women in particular:

Alison Adcock	Dinah Freeman
Liz Banks	Daphne Green
Sally Barnes	Margaret Hall
Carol Barker Bennett	Margaret Lowes
Dr Margaret Birch	Gillian Lunn
Pamela Bome	Anne Malins
B. Broomfield	Margaret Mallett
Honor J. M. Coales	Margaret Orrell
Yvonne Craig	Alison Phillips
Sara Crowley	Valerie Powell
Patricia Dawson	Maggie Redding
Margaret Daye	Anne Ring
Tina Everett	Evelyn Swales
Valerie Ferguson	Mrs Ward

For all that neophyte authors owe to a superlative editor, we thank John Bowden. For important commentary on the text we are most grateful to Dr Pamela Tudor-Craig, Ruth McCurry and Valerie Flessati. For Linda's awakening to political consciousness we thank Joan Baez. Frances Charles taught Susan to look theologically at women and the world, and continues to do so – *Laus Deo*. For continual spiritual sustenance we thank Una and Leo Kroll.

We dedicate this book to our children: Barnaby, Benjamin, Caitlin, Clare, Dominic and Sean. To our husbands Graham and Tom. And to each other in sisterly love.

Preface to the Second Edition

We wrote *Dispossessed Daughters of Eve* as an attempt to bridge, for ourselves and for the reader, what we saw as a formidable gulf. On one side stood the Church, our Church, dimly aware of a 'woman problem' it needed to address; on the other side was the immense energy, restlessness and longing for change among Christian women. It seemed that the Church had not even begun to perceive or reflect on the source and meaning of a women's movement which had brought about profound change in the lives of women everywhere.

This gulf became apparent in the 1970s as the Anglican Church worldwide prepared to re-open the question of women's ordination to the priesthood. As we prepared and wrote this book, we were encouraged by the increasing numbers of women applying to study theology in order to ready themselves for pastoral and teaching ministries. 'Professional' and lay Christian women like ourselves were meeting, formally and informally, to pray, campaign for women's ordination, sing and tell stories. Together we were charting women's experience in Christianity past and present, seen through the critical perspective of Western feminism. The General Synod debate itself, in 1978/9 (see chapter 5, pp. 70–2), made clear the nature and depth of (clerical) resistance to women's full participation in the ministry and mission of the Christian Churches. While on one level we were outraged at the widely expressed idea that the Church was 'not ready' for women's priestly ministry, it quickly became obvious that achieving the goal of priesthood could not, and *should* not, happen without a broadly based campaign of education in the deep theological issues involved.

Dispossessed Daughters of Eve was the first full-length British offering in the growing field of feminist theological enquiry. As we had hoped, a good deal of widespread, useful discussion followed the book's publication in 1981. It served to reinforce a growing public awareness that the ordination issue was only the tip of the iceberg; an iceberg, we are told in this current round of the debate, which will split the ship. Ours was a preliminary sounding. And we hope today, as we hoped when we wrote the book, that it will encourage further exploration. Many such explorations are now widely available. Women writers have given illuminated, finely tuned readings of our submerged history and traditions. Margaret Hebblethwaite's account of God, seen as and through the Mother (*Motherhood and God*, Geoffrey Chapman 1984), and Elizabeth Schüssler Fiorenza's scholarly feminist reconstruction of our earliest Christian origins, *In Memory of Her* (SCM Press 1983), are but two examples of the depth and range of women's theological thinking today.

In this preface to the second edition of our own book we will attempt to outline some of the ways in which the gulf between the Church and women is closing. There are real signs that the Church is taking serious note of the insights of the women's and other liberation movements; signs, too, that 'secular' feminists are increasingly sympathetic to the spiritual dimensions of women's experience. But we must not allow the optimism engendered by this to blind us to the hardened hearts and minds we discern among people and institutions which wield real power in our everyday lives. We are concerned, here and in our original text, to point to some alarming retrenchments, political and religious, which stunt growth and reject the ways of the Spirit to change and heal.

Entrenchment and polarization are painfully apparent in the current reversals of the procedure towards women's ordination, and this is reflected in the media presentation of the issue. Over the last five years or so numerous radio and television programmes have regularly shown interest in the subject of women in the Churches. Some of these programmes have come to demonstrate a profound grasp of the underlying issues and history of the ordination struggle. A good example is Angela Tilby's *God is She* (made for the *Everyman* TV series and shown on 20 October 1985), which portrayed a quintet of Christian women's reflections on the roles assigned to them in Christian tradition. They were cast, arbitrarily, as the producer confessed, as mother, nun, reformer, teacher and writer, and given space to present their own personal and intellectual critique of Christianity's misogynistic traditions. Three of these women, the nun, the teacher and the reformer, were active proponents of women's ordination.

That same month, ITV's *Heart of the Matter* looked at the specific question of women's ordination. Deaconess Frances Foster, the young woman who was the main 'pro' participant in this programme, was treated in striking contrast to the women mentioned above. She was constantly questioned as to how she, in asking the Church to test her priestly vocation, could reconcile herself to the 'pain' felt by priests who opposed women's ordination. No such question was asked of the priest in the 'anti' corner of this programme. It seems to be necessary, when presenting a woman offering the Church not only her mind but her whole *self* as a priest or minister, that she run the all-too-familiar gauntlet of her (minority) clerical opponents. This is called media 'balance'. The net result, in Frances Foster's case, was that the audience was given no chance to get to know *her*, her unique gifts and thoughts, at all! This approach, though tiresome, nevertheless accurately portrays the political realities of the situation. Synodical procedure, which insists on a two-thirds majority in all three houses, ensures that the power of veto on any institutional changes stays firmly in the hands of those few who remain determinedly deaf to what women in the churches are actually thinking and saying.

When we first began to write this book we were frequently made to feel by our secular feminist friends that the patriarchal roots and structures of the Church were of little relevance to those outside. It was 'our problem' if we chose to remain within organized religion. This stance was confirmed by the areas of research given importance and priority in the writings of the 1970s' women's movement (see pp. 2–3 of *Dispossessed Daughters*). That this gulf is now closing is a tribute to the openness and honesty of both 'sides', as well as being a source of strength and nourishment: feminist theology is now immeasurably enriched by the insights and erudition of a whole range of feminist writing.

This new openness to spirituality as a real and necessary concern of the feminist movement was signalled by the feminist publishing house Virago, when in 1983 they brought out a collection entitled *Walking on the Water: Women Talk about Spirituality* (Garcia and Maitland). Today, our daughters have at their disposal a worldwide compendium of popular writing specifically concerned with recovering women's spiritual roots and strength. A fictional bestseller of 1985/6 was *Mists of Avalon* by Marion Zimmer-Bradley (Sphere 1984), a magical, beautiful retelling of the Arthurian legends from the standpoint of Morgan La Fay. Morgan, Arthur's half-sister, Mistress of Magic, has previously always been the villainess, invoking the Dark Gods to wreak havoc and destruction in the Christian court. Zimmer-Bradley's book is a powerful condemnation of religious exclusivism, of the Christian missionaries' stamping out of the older Celtic religion which honoured women as the creators of life and the keepers of Wisdom.

Marina Warner, whose monumental study of the Virgin, *Alone of all her Sex* (paperback Pan Books 1985), was a crucial and formative inspiration ten years ago, continues to explore the tensions and contradictions between female heroism and the historical workings of male-structured culture. Her study *Joan of Arc* (Weidenfeld and Nicolson 1981) gives us a more rounded, dynamic Joan than the saint and patriot we have inherited, and it

> . . . is intended as a plea. In the writing of female biography it is easy to revert unconsciously to known stereotypes. Joan of Arc is a pre-eminent heroine because she belongs to the sphere of action, while so many feminine figures or models are assigned or confined to the sphere of contemplation. She is anomalous in our culture, a woman renowned for doing something on her own, not by birthright. She has extended the taxonomy of female types . . . It is urgent that this taxonomy be expanded and that the multifarious duties that women have historically undertaken be recognised, researched and named. Like Eskimos who enjoy a rich lexicon of many different words for snow, we must develop a richer vocabulary for female activity than we [have] at present, with our restrictions of wife, mother, mistress, muse. Joan of Arc, in all her brightness, illuminates the operation of our present classification system, its rigidity on the one hand, its potential on the other.

This expansion of taxonomy is something that has been happening in definitions of sexuality. We owe an apology to lesbian women for implying (in chapter 3) that their lifestyle derives mainly from a hatred and rejection of men. One of the many perceptions emerging from lesbian analysis is that all previous definitions of human sexuality are male-derived, and these definitions are too narrow. This observation is important and far reaching.

Another important milestone on the home front of Christian feminism was Sara Maitland's contribution in 1983, *A Map of the New Country* (Routledge and Kegan Paul). Here Sara turns from her established crafts of fiction writing and journalism to survey the implications of feminist theory and practice for women in the Churches. Researched and published on both sides of the Atlantic, this book is bigger and broader in scope than our own. Ours is more domestic, more pastoral perhaps, written for 'the woman in the pew'. Sara's ambivalence in the book about the value of women's ordination – although it caused some pain at the time – seems in retrospect to have made a creative contribution to the debate as things stand today. She is passionately – and prophetically – concerned to emphasize the dangers of 'over-investing' in ordination, and the considerable pressures towards co-option into a male model of priesthood. She declares that Sisterhood as a 'model that is becoming a historical, material reality . . . is our service, our ministry, our collective *vocation* [italics ours]. That model must not be compromised for small gains from a bankrupt bureaucracy.'

Sara, whose commitment to feminism pre-dated her conversion to Christianity, has been in a unique position to understand and address the aforementioned mutual lack of communication between 'secular' and religious feminism. This was more marked in Britain and took longer to break down than in the USA. The reasons for this are important as we come to assess what we believe to be a new cohesiveness and creativity in the feminist enterprise. As we discuss in chapter 1, nineteenth-century feminism, as it arose in the USA, went hand-in-hand with the anti-slavery movement – and female religious zeal was a prominent feature of both. The reforming endeavours of British women (see pp. 10–11) have been more easily underplayed in our history and culture; their work more easily seen as merging into a longer and more formal nineteenth-century reforming process. This century, the British women's movement has been informed by a much harsher Marxist critique of society than the US movement, which has always laid greater stress on cultural and careerist issues. The situation in the Churches has been different, too. In the USA, the spectrum of radical/conservative has always cut across Church and society. In the Churches of Britain, male radicals have been far slower to take the questions raised by feminists seriously: the lack of feminist interest in the Churches was echoed by a corresponding deafness from the Churches about the women's movement. Being a Christian and a feminist was tough going ten years ago!

Christian feminists have worked very hard, as has the Western women's movement as a whole, to create national and international bases and networks where our particular histories can be aired and shared. The national groups listed in our text have grown apace and new ones have arisen to meet new needs. The Movement for the Ordination of Women (MOW), set up in 1979, was in its infancy when our book went to press. Since then MOW has worked and published to highlight 'a debate of which the narrow end, as it were, is the ordination of women to the priesthood and the broad end is the full evaluation of women within the Christian community and maybe within society as a whole', to quote ex-Moderator Monica Furlong's introduction to MOW's symposium *Feminine in the Church* (SPCK 1984).

MOW is committed to work for canonical change, for openness and genuine grass roots debate in the Church. Its undoubted success in this aim has led to the earlier-than-hoped-for reintroduction of the matter onto the Synod's agenda. 'MOW found itself somewhat to its own surprise becoming an influence in the Church, as its numbers soared beyond the usual membership of church organisations. It was clear it was tapping a new source of energy, that it had a dynamism not often seen in the Church of England', writes Monica Furlong. MOW's optimism and openness (much needed and sorely tried of late) was based on far more than success at the opinion polls; it was fuelled by a dramatically increased awareness of the underlying, fundamental issues involved. MOW itself has made a substantial contribution to this increased awareness in its public campaign.

There have, of course, been the usual interior tensions, inevitable in such a broad-based movement. The more radical Christian feminists have often chafed under the discipline of MOW's determined reformist/gradualist approach; the gentler, more mannerly members have often been startled and dismayed at the irreverence and impatience of the radicals. But the tension has been a creative one, we believe. MOW has pursued its aims without stifling a radical critique of the institution of the Church.

This claim, that MOW has successfully held a balance, can be upheld by the fact that its critics and enemies have simultaneously accused it of radical subversiveness and obsessive churchiness! The former accusation runs through William Oddie's book *What Will Happen to God?* (SPCK 1984), which collapses the entire spectrum of Christian feminism into the category of embittered militancy. Woe to you when all (such) men speak good of you!

To MOW a daughter, WIT (Women in Theology), born 1983/4. WIT's aims are 'to advance the theological education of women and the training of women to the priesthood and, in so doing, to draw out and make available to both women and men, theological insights'. WIT has not limited its vision to training for the formal priesthood, but works to build bridges between the institution and its more radical critics, to train women for whatever model of ministry should be called forth in the future Church.

In November 1984, General Synod voted in favour of drawing up the necessary legislation for women's ordination in the UK. The erstwhile 'road-block' of the two-thirds clerical majority (see pp. 70–80 and p. 139, note 2, of *Dispossessed Daughters*) had been negotiated on this occasion. Progress made in this 'clergy conversion' area of MOW's work is gratifying and interesting. Many clergy who had previously voted for progressive/radical synodical motions on issues like South Africa and nuclear weapons, but against women priests in 1978, were no longer doing so. They were taking serious note of a changed consciousness in the churches as a whole, and were now convinced that the time was ripe. Six years of Thatcher had sharpened up the liberals and the left.

But now a concerted rearguard action from the ecclesiastical right has orchestrated a series of damaging blows, bringing about the reversals of July 1986. To begin with, we have been treated to Tory parliamentarian obstruction on technical grounds of the long-overdue measure allowing women to be made deacons, i.e. enter holy orders. The *Church Times* commented (17 October 1986) on the 'anxiety that it may fall foul of the many MPs who are angry with the Church for taking what they regard as an anti-Government stand on various issues'.

A further blow was the defeat again (as in July 1979) of the motion allowing women priests from overseas to function in Britain. This ruling was the one most likely to be challenged by 'illegal' action by clergy and parishes disgusted with this imperialist stance by the 'mother' Church. On 4 October 1986 one such 'illegal' celebration hit the headlines. The Reverend Joyce Bennett, ordained in Hong Kong in 1971, celebrated the Eucharist for MOW members after their 1986 AGM in Church House.

Finally, the whole matter of women's ordination was removed from Synod's agenda and handed back to the bishops to determine further action. This last came about as the result of a group being appointed by Synod to examine the scope and content of the legislation needed to remove the legal barriers preventing the ordination of women. Heavily weighted towards protecting those clergy and laity who cannot accept women priests, the report's recommendations have appalled and dismayed many people, on both sides of the debate. Procedures were suggested to allow parishes to 'lock out' their bishop, i.e. refuse to accept his episcopal ministrations if they disapprove of the bishop concerned having ordained a woman, or, presumably of having received her priestly ministry as Bishop Peter Selby of Kingston did at the MOW Eucharist. We are right back here, it feels, in the language of female uncleanness, a kind of reversal of the idea of apostolic succession: a bishop laying hands on a woman receives her impurity and is 'unclean' himself.

Generous financial provisions were proposed for those clergy who would be forced, in conscience, to resign their orders: up to ten years' salary and money for housing. Such 'consciences' like to see themselves as inheriting the mantle of St Thomas More and others, who paid for their defence of the Old Faith with their heads. What have we come to? Martyrdom on £5,000 per annum in a three-bedroomed semi! It is outrageous that such an image of Christian ministry, based on privilege and safeguards, is being presented to the world.

Threats of schism and synodical set-backs are bitterly disappointing, but we are constantly challenged by the gospel itself, and by listening and learning from one another, to keep our own parochial and cultural concerns in perspective. Women from the Third World, women of colour in our own society, speak to us of a triple struggle with poverty, colonialism and sexist oppression. In order to hear these voices, we are learning to organize our meetings in different ways from the customary conference/seminar formats. This is vitally important for the inter-faith, inter-cultural exchanges that have begun to take place among women. A good example is a women's gathering at Harvard University, in Boston, USA in 1984, which was smaller and much longer than is common for this sort of international event. Western feminists played a deliberately low-key role so that women from other religious traditions (at this meeting it was mainly Jewish, Asian, Arab and black women who set the agenda) could articulate the bitter and perplexing conflicts between their respective political groupings, and so move towards a common feminist ethic.

We wish to pay tribute in this preface to the work done by Rosemary Radford Ruether. Her work as a founding Mother of US feminist theology was a major inspiration to us when we wrote this book. She has continued to contribute to this theme in her writing and teaching, and she is also a tireless weaver of feminist networks, generously and creatively putting her international platform and stature at our disposal. Her visits to Britain were the focus for an important conference, 'Women, Men and Power', held in King's College London in 1983, and for the setting up of the Catholic Women's Network (UK) in 1984. She has co-edited a three-volume documentary history of women and religion in the US and works hard to stimulate a parallel project here. In the summer of 1986 she came to do some research on the history of Quaker Women in Britain and ran an open course of seminars for women at Heythrop (RC) College.

As feminist theology emerged first and most full-bloodedly in the US, so also has the backlash against it and against women's rights generally. Since 1983 the Equal Rights Amendment has failed in the US, a failure which would have seemed inconceivable a few years before. US reports tell us that certain sections of the Churches in Reagan's America are extensively funding and orchestrating this ultra-right repression. In her address to the 'Women, Men and Power' conference, Ruether drew out the connections between traditional religious ideologies defining women as defective and subordinate and the secular ideologies of the New Right.

In Britain, women's particular health and welfare needs are where the cuts are applied most deeply and damagingly. Women's job opportunities also suffer heavily in the present recession. As in the US, a virulent new strain of patriarchal conservatism, calling itself the pro-family lobby, reinforces these depressing developments. A conjunction of Thatcher supporters and Christians 'concerned' for the family (i.e. a right-wing appropriation of family and personal morality) was formally proposed in the pages of the *Church Times* in March 1986. This development is of particular

concern for Christian women, who can so easily find themselves
brought in on the side of arguments for women's 'traditional' role
in society, and thereby used to promote repressive policies.

This assertion, made by many contemporary feminists, is one
which bears serious examination. It is not, we believe, an unjust
one to level even at a Church which is often openly critical of the
hard-line Toryism of this present Government. Prominent church
critics of monetarist policies and cuts in public spending need to
be more sharply aware both of the ways in which present trends
are promoted as upholding 'traditional Christian values' and of
the ways they harm women particularly, for these two phenomena
are deeply interwoven.

For example, cuts in nursery school places and in hospital beds
for patients needing long-term care put heavy burdens on women,
on whom care for the very young, the old and the infirm inevitably
falls. 'Community care' is the State's euphemism for the withdrawal
of welfare services. But this Government is also openly committed
to reasserting women's place in the home, as part of its pro-family
stance and to make the unemployment figures look better; although
of course a stay-home wife is unaffordable for poorer families.

It is this same domestic role which the Church upholds in its
teaching. In theory, the Church proclaims the servant/nurturer role
as mandatory for Christians of both sexes, and traditional
wifehood/motherhood as a particular vocation – that is, a choice
freely embraced – for some women. But in practice, certainly in
the day-to-day running of parish life, this is not upheld. It is women
who are expected to perform the more menial tasks vaunted as
truly feminine. Another euphemism for enclosure in the domestic
sphere. So the feminists' catchphrase of 'the combined forces of
Church and State' as powerful sources of women's oppression is
pertinent indeed when both *seem* in accord in imposing limitations
on women's public value and potential. Christian men of goodwill
and lay women, serene in the tasks the Church offers them, would
do well to reflect on how truly fragile and vulnerable traditional
femininity and traditional family values are under the combined
forces of monetarism and militarism.

As has been pointed out earlier, the barriers in Britain between
secular and religious feminism have been more rigid than in the
US. However, as these break down it becomes possible for us to
draw strength from the socialist/dissident roots of British feminism.
It seems increasingly likely that the political experience of valuing

and defending institutions like the Welfare State, the right of all to health care, and the whole pre-eminently practical approach that has characterized feminist endeavour in this country, will be our most valuable offering to the growing international bases of Christian feminism. This tradition might prove particularly useful to women in the United States, where feminist thinking and strategy has laid possibly too much emphasis on 'playing the system', on being successful in 'a man's world' rather than on social critique – and where socialism is a dirty word and Marx unmentionable in polite company!

The coincidence of our book being published four months before the walk by Women for Life on Earth from Cardiff to Greenham Common in September 1981 (and *not* back again) confirmed the sense of our final chapter. Greenham has marked a new departure in peace activism and feminist prophecy. Many Christian women have joined the camp at Greenham; we and our friends spend time there when we can. In recognition of the hope and inspiration given us by the women of Greenham, Christian women have begun the Greenham vigil, which includes an hourly liturgy and night-watch. Angela West from the Oxford Women's Group constructed the liturgy for the vigil, based on Mark's Gospel, and published an article (in *New Blackfriars*, March 1986) entitled 'Greenham Vigil – A Christian Women's Theological Initiative for Peace'. West's article explored the spiritual significance of a continuing tradition of radical obedience and bodily witness:

> As Christians, we may consider the peace camp as standing in line with the works of the prophets. But the camp may also speak to us of the New Testament part of our tradition. It may serve to remind us of our fundamental vocation as Christians – the call to live in the body of Christ and to share in the fate of that body . . . For us, the consciousness of being one body begins as it began for the early church – with fear for our lives. The witness of the women at Greenham recalls the witness of those other women in first-century Palestine who kept their vigil at the foot of the Cross. In joining the vigil, we are joining our stories to this story . . . we link our personal essays in freedom to the struggles of those across the world who suffer oppression, and acknowledge a common bond with them in our hope for liberation from the gods of war.

When we first became involved with the issue of the ordination of women, and as we prepared to write this book, we were often told that the Church had far more important things to deal with; an argument repeated this year by the Archbishop of Canterbury to a delegation from MOW. Now we are told how schismatic, divisive and dangerous the issue is. These threats have created a climate of paranoia and misapprehension of the question. Vociferous opponents show no sign of having heard what the pro-ordination lobby, or Christian feminism in general, is actually saying.

A new group has been formed called Women Against the Ordination of Women. This group's four-page advertising feature, published in the *Church Times* (summer 1986), has brought the debate to an unprecedented low. Page one announces that 'this is a relatively new theological question', a staggering assertion in the light of history. The issue has been under practical debate for a hundred years, leaving aside the fact that the place of women was clearly a live issue in the early Church, as very clearly recorded in the New Testament. 'The terrible demoralisation of people from top to bottom' of the US Episcopal Church is invoked as an argument by one contributor; by another, the old chestnut that equality is synonymous with 'interchangeability'. Most worrying of all is the statement picked out in heavy black letters: 'God is not *like* our Father. He *is* our Father. We have no need to address him as "mother".' Have these writers not read the Gospels, where Jesus himself likens the divine to a mother hen? Have they not learned in classroom or confirmation class that both Old and New Testament alike teach that all descriptions of God are analogical, and that to absolutize a human word or image is to break the second commandment? All this in defence of orthodoxy and 'tradition'!

So, in many ways the gulf between the current debate about ordination and the reality of our lives and concerns is ever widening. The time is out of joint. The question we ask at the end of this book, 'Why bother?' (p. 113), is unchanging and ever more urgent. The answer rests, as it always did, in the elements of biblical faith which are all over the world being reclaimed.

Claiming the priesthood for women today is a fundamentally different undertaking from the campaign of the late 1970s. Then, we were asking the Church to catch up with a revived feminism that was the coming thing. The arguments were inevitably weighted towards the advances women had made in the modern world and the gifts they had been shown to possess. In the late 1980s we call upon the Church not only to repent of its sexism and be forgiven, but also, now, to be prophetic in a dark time. After all, the Church of England has, in the last few years, stood up against a veritable bonanza backlash over *The Church and the Bomb*, the controversial Falkland's thanksgiving service in 1982, monetarism, and most recently has taken a firm stand on economic sanctions against the apartheid regime of South Africa. As MOW's Monica Furlong once quipped, 'there's life in the old bitch yet!'

Speaking for ourselves, we have learnt from our involvement in local and national campaigns for peace and justice that it is a mistake to see the ordination issue as 'domestic'. Recent developments in the Church itself give the lie to talk about 'more pressing concerns'. Our own understanding of prophecy and the meaning of incarnation – making real, fleshly and vulnerable the means of spiritual truth – draws us to develop a bifocal vision, in which our feminist experience informs and respects the mundane, tedious struggle for justice and equality in the torn and flawed fabric of the Church. And vice versa.

Linda continues to teach at the American School in London and to live in London's East End, where she works on local peace and ecology issues. She has recently completed editing a book on women's sexuality and spirituality (*Sex and God: Some Varieties of Women's Religious Experience*, Routledge and Kegan Paul, April 1987).

Susan has written an essay on monogamy for Linda's book. Her most recent writing has been for peace movement publications. She has written on the ecological dimensions of world peace in Christian CND's booklet *In God We Trust* (from CND Publications, 22–24 Underwood Street, London N1, £1.95). She is the editor of *Focus on Peace and Justice*, Kevin Mayhew Ltd, Suffolk.

We both continue to write, teach and hope.

1

Daughters of the Enlightenment

'Eve', *see* 'Adam' (*New Hutchinson's Twentieth Century Encyclopedia*, revised and enlarged for the 1980s).

Feminism: 'Advocacy of rights and equality of women in social, economic and political spheres, a commitment to the fundamental alteration of women's role in society' (*Fontana Dictionary of Modern Thought*).

'Mother, may I go out to swim?'
'Yes, my darling daughter;
Hang your clothes on a hickory limb
But don't go near the water' (Anon).

*   *   *

Apollo, God of light and of rational thought (in fact, one of his other names is Loxias – the Word) is said to have appeared to the Trojan princess Cassandra and promised her his gift of prophecy if she would lie with him. Cassandra accepted Apollo's gift and promised her body to him. When the time came for her to fulfil that promise, she was terrified of Apollo's great heat and light and went back on the bargain. Apollo, angered, took away not his gift of prophecy, but Cassandra's credibility, condemning her, until her death, always to see the truth and tell it, but ensuring that no one would ever believe what she prophesied.

Cassandra is our sister and our symbol. Poised somewhere between the age-old figure of the nagging woman and the more tragi-romantic descriptions of female obscurity – the many flowers 'born to blush unseen' – she serves as a parable of women's absence from cult and history-making.

Children in school are told tales of kings and heroes; the unsung heroes who did not make the pages of the books are, even the most troublesome of them, deemed to be part of a large cast of extras. Their obscurity is often described in such noble terms as 'village

Hampdens' if they did their stuff or 'gentlemen in England now abed' who 'think themselves accursed they were not here', if they missed out on history-making. Women, though, fulfil the great enterprises of history *by* their invisibility, unless by some quirk of birth or fate they are required to lay aside their womanly yearnings and take on a sacrificial mantle of tortured destiny. Violets by mossy stones are part of the natural order, and Cassandras have to be set aside for the proper business of slaughter and revenge to roll forward the rise and decline of great civilizations.

Feminist history begins with a recognition and acknowledgment of this process. We take great comfort from our discovery that the women's movement is much older than we would have previously imagined. We are heartened to see (and the more we read the more we do indeed see) that the flowering of women's consciousness of their own innate value as persons cannot be confined to sociological description any more than it can be confined to what we arrogantly imagine to be modern enlightenment or discernible periods.

If historical feminism has been a neglected part of mainstream historical treatment, historical religious feminism has been almost totally ignored. Yet recent research[1] indicates that religious feminists were critically important in the progress towards abolition and myriad social reforms as well as suffrage in the nineteenth century.

Today there is a mutual lack of communication between mainstream religious thinking and secular feminism. The literature of women's studies in this country virtually ignores the category of 'Women and Religion'. A recent guide to the literature of the women's movement, claimed to be the first comprehensive guide, contains sections on domestic life, paid work, health, education and welfare, law and politics, crime and deviance, literature, art and popular culture, cross-cultural studies, social and psychological perspectives, additional bibliographies.[2] The notable absence of 'religion and women' is by no means accidental; for the majority of secular feminists, the study of women and religious institutions is peripheral.

We hope in this chapter to trace briefly the historical reasons for this split and, in our book as a whole, to give some arguments for the incorporation of feminist vision in the life of the church. The assumption we work with is that most women currently writing about feminism are alienated from institutional religion and, although recognizing the role of the church in a long history of sexist repression, have little doctrinal understanding of this process. A serious gap thus exists in understanding the dilemmas of the women's movement.

Religion has not simply been a peripheral phenomenon to be understood only in negatives. It is without doubt the single most important shaper and enforcer of women's image and role in culture and society. This recognition holds true whether one has a dialectical/economic view of history or a psychological 'male-struggle-for-freedom-from-Mom (alias nature)' view. Either way, religion has been the symbolic reflection and provided ethical ballast for female subjugation and sexual apartheid. Although the women's movement no longer ignores religion, women who uphold the Christian gospel are obliged to clarify its message, name the distortions of its followers, and cease to patronize their secular sisters who have only experienced the reality of the latter.

It seems crucial from our vantage point to see where the divergences between religious and secular feminism developed and deepened. To this end we want to sketch the phenomenon of Western feminism with some restorative emphasis on its theological inspiration. There is no better way to limit our list than to discuss the people who have in our own lives taken hold of our imagination.

The women of our rough chronology have taught us something important about ourselves as well as the movement.

They are the privileged and articulate, the touchstones of the movement. We recognize the anomaly of using a version of history which women are attempting to shed; nevertheless, such lives are a valuable legacy. Literature is the only intellectual field to which privileged women over a long stretch of time have made an irreplaceable contribution. The fight for political justice and equality ricochets off the volatile workings of political and social history, but all the time, all the time the women wrote – sometimes as polemicists, sometimes as literary feminists, conscious or unconscious. We mourn the countless women whose voices were not heard, the 'mute inglorious Miltons' who may or may not have chosen to subscribe to that poet's strictures about woman's place; we content ourselves simply to rejoice in those who were heard.

The impulse to politicized female protest undoubtedly came from the doctrines and philosophies that inspired the French Revolution and received further impetus from the economic changes wrought by the Industrial Revolution as a whole. Women's Clubs were set up in the France of 1789, and feminist tracts were circulated in abundance. The grievances of working women were particularly acute. They were, as one pamphlet put it, 'the Third Estate of the Third Estate'.[3] These pamphlets, and the hot issue of women's estate as clarified and debated by the polemicist Condorcet, were primarily responsible for the voices of women being articulated and heard properly in Europe.

It was to the voices of the French Revolution and the French feminists of the late eighteenth century that the great Mary Wollstonecraft (1759–1797) responded. Like most lettered women of her time, Mary was largely self-taught. It was partly her continuing association with political radicals who were also theological radicals, combined with the ideals of Liberty, Equality and Fraternity, that fired her imagination and evolved into her splendid *Vindication of the Rights of Woman*. Her most influential religious associates were Dr Richard Price, moral theologian, whose sermon 'On Love of Country', delivered in 1789, prompted Edmund Burke's *Reflections on the French Revolution*; Joseph Priestley, publisher of *History of Early Opinions Concerning Jesus Christ* in 1786; and not least Mary's husband William Godwin, who showed continuing interest in religious, albeit strange and occult, practices.

Published in 1792, the *Vindication* was little noticed at first. Wollstonecraft set out in this book no less than the entirety of the feminist ideal in her declaration of female independence and equality. In her book, Mary presented the first known and sustained argument for female emancipation based on a cogent ethical system. Her central argument runs thus: women's fate, as conceived by male-dominated society, makes nothing more than 'mere animals of them'. They are conditioned to subdue their gifts and energy to a central life task of achieving and sustaining as materially beneficial and secure a marriage as possible. Women's education is structured to this end. Female intellect is valued or tolerated only in so far as it enhances and does not impede the process of feminization and desirable docility. Mary Wollstonecraft concluded that the vast majority of earlier writing made light of women's capacities or honoured women for the very qualities that make them untrustworthy. If women could share the rights and opportunities of men and be freed from economic dependence, they would then be able to claim and contribute the virtues of courage and magnanimity. Half the world's untapped human resources would be released and the perfectability of man – a revolutionary doctrine which Mary whole-heartedly embraced – would be a nearer-realized dream.

Her essential message that women are human beings before they are sexual beings did not lead Mary to scorn men. Woman's perfectability is inextricable from man's, and strong parental love is an essential part of the promised covenant. She favoured early marriage and despised the 'wild oats' sexual experimentation that she realistically knew to lead to callous exploitation of young working-class girls and the acceptance of double standards. Wollstonecraft frowned on the practice of farming young children out to nurses and sending them away to school. She favoured co-educational day schools as a way of curbing the power of external authority structures. Only the warmth and nurture of a democratic home could provide an authority worthy of respect and able to undermine both anarchy and the materialism that Mary saw as the source of all tyranny, presaging the 'small is beautiful' philosophy of our own day. Mary's political radicalism rejected all hierarchies – military, ecclesiastical and social. Like her descendent sisters, Mary saw female oppression to be inextricable from class and race oppression and likened women to all subject classes and slaves. They are property and 'from the respect paid to property flow as from a poisoned fountain, most of the evils and vices which render this world such a dreary scene to the contemplative mind'.[4]

Despite her devastating critique of society, Mary Wollstonecraft's book is neither extremist nor angry. She genuinely felt herself to be liberated. Despite great hardship and deep personal pain and rejection – she twice attempted suicide – her undaunted spirit was remarkable and pervades the lofty idealism of her book. 'For my arguments, Sir, are debated by a disinterested spirit – I plead for my sex, not for myself. Independence I have long considered the grand blessing of my life, the basis of every virtue – and independence I will ever secure, though I were to live on a barren heath.'[5]

One can trace a definite Wollstonecraft tradition in subsequent feminist demand. Mary considered all aspects of women's condition – economic, cultural, psychological – as interrelated, with effective reform dependent on basic social change in the redistribution of political and economic power. All modern feminists, radical or conservative, religious or secular, are Wollstonecraft's philosophical descendants.

Wollstonecraft's contemporaries called her a shameless wanton, a 'philosophizing serpent', one of the 'impious Amazons of Republican France'. Horace Walpole referred to her as a 'hyena in petticoats'. Other virulent detractors recommended that her life and work be read 'with disgust by every female who has any pretensions to delicacy; with detestation by everyone attached to the interests of religion and morality, and with indignation by anyone who might feel regard for the unhappy woman, whose frailities should have been buried in oblivion'. After her death, Bishop Percy of Dromore capitalized on rumours of scandal and incest in Mary's past in order to discredit her, and another Irish bishop preached a sermon linking Voltaire and Mary Wollstonecraft Godwin in infamy.[6]

Mary Wollstonecraft died of septicaemia following the birth of her second child, Mary (who survived to become the author of *Frankenstein* and wife to the poet Shelley). In her excellent biography,[7] Claire Tomalin comments that Mary's death at the end of the eighteenth century symbolized the death of the bravado and robust optimism that had characterized the age. Many of Mary's radical associates were to retrench their views and submit to the caution and prudery of the succeeding century.

The feminist movement was most cruelly crushed in France, its birthplace. The Women's Clubs, after a life of four years, were abolished by Robespierre in the autumn of 1793. Mary Wollstonecraft's French counterpart was Olympe de Gouges. In 1791 she published her *Declaration of the Rights of Woman* in answer to the Rights of Man proclaimed by the Constituent Assembly two years before. She was guillotined in 1793 for attacking the perpetrators of the Terror. The Code Napoleon upheld traditional patterns of male domination. Condorcet, in hiding, stayed faithful to the end and continued to assert that women's liberation and progress towards civilization were eternally inextricable. Such brief glory and bitter disappointment will radicalize any movement, and French feminism flourished underground during what was, in England and America, a time of quiescence. English and American feminists who had heard the revolutionary voices had no calls to martyrdom. Furthermore, a devastating European war, not for the first or the last time, frightened men and women back from the brink of revolutionary endeavour into status-quo political theory and conventional morality.

The movement was to gather steam once again in the mid-nineteenth century, both in England and America. The philosophical debate about women at this time was conducted by male philosophers. John Stuart Mill and William Lecky published diametrically opposed views of woman. Lecky propounded the cult of true womanhood and asserted the notion of women's moral superiority, which was both the rationale and the acceptable face of Victorian repressiveness. In 1869, Mill published *The Subjection of Women*,[8] a statement of robust feminist conviction, but his was essentially a lone voice.

To trace the overtly feminist convictions of the great women of the age, one has to look to their private disclosures in letters and conversations. Women like the Brontes and George Eliot poured their passions and energy into their novels. Some of these novels were considered quite shocking enough to the delicate sensibilities of their contemporaries but continue to disappoint their more activist sisters to this day. The soul and ear of Bronte and Eliot were so sensitively attuned to the universality of patriarchal power; realism demanded that their brave creations submit or be destroyed. George Eliot did create women who defied the household gods, but the small boats who braved the tempest were either dashed to pieces on the rocks, like Maggie Tulliver in *The Mill on the Floss*, or sailed to the safe haven of the Happy Ending and put down anchor in domesticity, as did Dorothea in *Middlemarch*: 'For there is no creature whose inward being is so strong that it is not greatly determined by what lies outside it.'[9]

Those women who did employ their pens in the service of polemic wrote pamphlets on a wide variety of urgent issues. By and large, the bulk of nineteenth-century feminist energy was concerned with the achievement of limited reforms – in the status of married women, in divorce legislation, labour laws, the ownership of property, the right to litigation and the move towards suffrage. The first champion of suffrage in England was Millicent Fawcett (1847–1929), who presented the first petition to Parliament in May 1867. When she arrived with a friend to make a public speech, the two women were referred to as 'ladies, wives of members of this house, who have disgraced themselves by speaking in public'.[10] She was not deterred and took her place in the subsequent widespread agitation as president of the large non-militant National Union of Women's Suffrage Societies, representing 500 to 600 non-militant groups pledged to 'unconditional co-operation with the government'.[11] Suffrage was finally realized in England in 1918, in the US in 1920, and in France (where demand had arisen earliest, in 1791), not until 1944.

In the struggle to dance round the edges of the central problem rather than to address its core lay the weakness and eventual inefficacy of nineteenth-century feminism. The attack on the institution of marriage by the more radical feminists and polemicists incurred the opprobrium of their more traditional reformist sisters as well as the wrath of all the churches except the Unitarians, Deists and 'free-thinkers'. Mainstream religious thought continued to avoid questioning the patriarchal context of its sexual ethic or to challenge the underlying assumptions on which the social order rested. The mid-century flavour of Anglican attitudes to women, even in its more enlightened circles, was wryly recorded by the newly-wed American Elizabeth Cady Stanton (see chapter 2), who attended the World Anti-Slavery Convention in London in 1840. Elected women delegates were relegated to the balcony behind a curtain and not allowed to speak – on the insistence of the clergy who claimed that 'women's subjection was divinely decreed when Eve was created'.[12] Her compatriot William Lloyd Garrison was one of the few men who registered his objection by sitting with the women. Mr Stanton did not support his wife.

While the campaign for women's suffrage remained conventionally reformist, the minority churches on both sides of the Atlantic did not hedge the questions that continued to gnaw at women. It was in the sectarian and holiness movements, offsprings of Methodism, that religious feminism developed and fed into secular feminism. Those men and women who remained in the mainstream churches may well have contributed to 'respectable' liberalist agitation, but thousands of the impatient and disenchanted found a home in the embryonic structures of Dissent. These myriad sects both sustained their feminist adherents and enabled radical feminist thought to continue to be fed by theological insight.

The Enlightenment feminist conviction that reason would lead to a progressively improved society, freed of ghosts and superstition, often led to extreme ideological stances. Some saw the church and its ally the state as the real villain, steeped in irrationality. A reasonable way to freedom, argued the rationalists, was the disestablishment of both institutions. But it was not just the atheist advocates of free love who gave feminism a bad name. The harridan image was often inspired by women whose overt sexual politics were moderate but who channelled their hostility to male-controlled society into such extremist activity as virulent teetotalism – smashing up bars[13] – and waging war against male sexuality. Curbing the immoderate lusts of 'the brutes' when one's eccentric dress and manner do not inspire it will render the crusader liable to scorn and laughter, but such extravagant behaviour at least had the value of protecting its perpetrators from the worst excesses of Victorian submissiveness. Any port in that particular storm of lies and sighing was not to be despised.

Great women like Elizabeth Cady Stanton did not, of course, withdraw commitment to the abolition cause because of its seating arrangements. Women of her ilk characterized an attitude to religion which was not innately suspicious but which was deeply critical of clericalism in particular and male domination of theology and biblical interpretation in general. The growth of mission agencies such as homes for unwed mothers, rescue missions, schools for training missionaries and social agencies for the poor was encouraged by the holiness and sectarian churches that contained the radical abolitionists and suffragists like Elizabeth Cady Stanton, Susan B. Anthony, Lucretia Mott and the Grimké sisters.[14] These ventures fulfilled needs that the established churches were not meeting and provided opportunities for female ministry that older churches had never met or soon abandoned. (The Methodist Conference had forbidden women to preach in the very early part of the century.)

After the American Civil War and the freeing of slaves, these churches seemed to lose the egalitarian thrust engendered by the drive for abolition. In moving from informal prayer meetings to formal associations, from sects to churches, the movement inevitably became caught up in the professionalizing of leadership. As Bible institutes and colleges associated with these groups became acceptable, higher academic degrees became a requirement at a time when few women were attaining them. Elizabeth Cady Stanton and Susan B. Anthony, her co-author of *The History of Women's Suffrage*, became alienated from their political and sectarian associates as these latter 'went respectable'.

The majority of religious feminists remained in the mainstream churches. These women have been called 'soft feminists'; they are women who have envisaged changes in the church and society but who have largely swallowed the social dictates of 'woman's place'. Such women sought to preserve traditional female virtues in a predominantly male social order. They saw their sphere as the care of children, the sick and disabled, and other women – even 'fallen' ones.

It was much more difficult for soft feminists than for hard feminists to remain aloof from the cult of True Womanhood. Summed up in the poetical image of the 'angel-in-the-house', women were exhorted to be patient and self-sacrificing. The vestal virgins of the cult were totally unequipped educationally, emotionally or even physically for women's real responsibilities within the family. Emphasis on fragility and doll-like docility – which was to rear its

well-coiffured head again in the nineteen fifties – gave no preparation for the stamina necessary for numerous pregnancies and the
rearing of large families. Working-class girls did not have to suffer
the cult's tortuous ritual and idolatry to the same extent. They and
their children were bred for the more functional aspects of Victorian social idealism – the expansionism that would require their
cheap labour. The poor woman had the double standard to contend
with ('She was poor but she was honest'), but once negotiated into
respectable marriage she was spared the widespread manifestations
of hysteria and 'the vapours' that beset and often killed her more
prosperous sisters.

While it is easy to understand how mainstream feminism went
'soft', lapsing into a more or less unquestioning moral tradition-
alism, it is nevertheless important to note the grim reality of the
sexual status quo that commanded such acquiescence and the price
paid by the poor for it. How strong must Josephine Butler have
been in her crusades against nineteenth-century hypocrisy! An Anglican, she is officially revered as the founder of Moral Welfare.[15]
The truth about her life is much grittier. She pointed out the
inter-relatedness of women's economic exploitation and their moral degradation. Her most courageous act was the formation of
working men's organizations to fight the Contagious Diseases Acts
of the 1860s. These Acts stipulated that any woman living in areas
close to military centres could be declared 'common prostitutes' by
the police and compelled to undergo medical examinations or go
to prison. Men were exempt. Josephine Butler physically attacked
the candidate who supported the Acts and was herself attacked by
mobs. Her efforts were rewarded by the repeal of the Acts in 1886.
She proved, too, that licensed brothels were thinly-disguised markets for white slave traffic and the sale of child prostitutes, and
influenced the government decision not to accept their proposed
licensing. Despite her efforts, by the end of the century the number
of women prostitutes in London alone was estimated at 80,000
(compared to the 8,000 of 1968s 'swinging London').[16]

Another young and ardent feminist, Catherine Mumford Booth,
found that her crusading spirit could not be contained by the
mainstream church. She persuaded her husband William to leave
the Methodist ministry and take to the high road. Catherine Booth
was primarily responsible for implanting sex equality into the
structures and work of the Salvation Army that she and William
founded in 1878.[17]

But the myth of True Womanhood persisted, and found a place

in even the most progressive Christian worship. The theological reflection of the 'feminization' of religious idealism revealed itself in increased interest in the suffering Christ and the 'Gentle Jesus meek and mild' hymns that became so popular. Such saccharine piety could not be expected to contain a spirit that had lived through the vagaries of the whole century, and women like Cady Stanton went out more and more on a limb. Soft feminists substituted the overtly political battles of abolitionism with the more pious and patronizing endeavours of the mission field. The split between hard feminism and religious zeal began to manifest itself. The daughters of the moral crusaders concentrated on consolidating rather than continuing the hard-won reforms of their parents. By their assent to the prevailing religious climate, many of the second generation retrenchers came to believe in some final headship of the husband which made it appropriate for them to contract crusade into good works, thus rendering it both respectable and unthreatening. 'Hard' and 'Soft' became indistinguishable.

While most religious feminists shied away from a fundamental examination of the church and family and their part in female oppression, the by-now-secularized radicals assumed that religion was dead and that the family was either on the wane or in urgent need of restructuring. The passions expended by their crusading forbears on religious issues were diverted into more hard-line political and economic analysis.

Our more complex perspective in the 1980s forces us to re-examine the Brave-New-World, glorious assumptions of secular Enlightenment thinking. We have come to recognize the continuing power of myth and aggression among people in both its negative and positive aspects. We have come to see that secularization and de-mythologizing have not created a more life-affirming world. We have trouble in summarily dismissing the importance of religious symbolism (even *bad* religious symbolism!) in our lives or in extolling the virtues of true rationality with as much confidence as, say, the Utopian socialists.

Frankly, the very term 'secularization of society' makes us itchy, since we are acutely aware of the extent to which people still respond to the symbolic messages that are meant to be communicated in religious language – and how often the hungry people are offered the stones of tradition instead of the sustenance of lively faith. We share the human despair at the failure of rationalism. Neither the church nor the state has discovered the secret of universal love. If there is a tidy way to conceptualize the second wave of feminism, it is in the understanding that there is a ghost in our well-oiled technological machine and that there is still something profoundly and *specifically* wrong for women.

The twentieth century opened, like its predecessor, with an unprecedented explosion of military conflict. The crippling effects of World War I scarcely need to be described. Leonard Woolf claimed that the nearly-grasped dream of Western and ultimately global civilization ended when the shots rang out at Sarajevo. Yet this time, the devastation preceded an immediate, unfaltering resurgence of feminism. The years immediately following this 'war to end all wars' saw the suffrage campaign satisfactorily concluded.[18] Mavericks like the marvellous anarchist Emma Goldman were ready for the next hurdle. Scornful of the spurious token of franchise, she insisted that the real battle for emancipation begins neither at the polls nor in court, but in a woman's soul (written in 1919).[19] Women must learn that freedom will extend only so far as their power to achieve it for themselves will reach. Feminists were urged to begin this inner regeneration by cutting loose from the constraints of prejudice, tradition and custom.

Post-war feminists were optimistic and energetic in their pursuit of education. Virginia Woolf addressed the 'daughters of educated men' in her essay *Three Guineas*,[20] posing the question that perplexes both ardent and sceptical feminists to this day. The early feminists assumed that the intellectual structure and contents of education available to men were viable, i.e. enduring, universal, civilizing to the mind and sensitizing to the spirit. Virginia Woolf takes issue:

> The questions that we have to ask and to answer about that procession during this moment of transition are so important that they may well change the lives of all men and women for ever. For we have to ask ourselves here and now: do we wish to join that procession or don't we? On what terms shall we join that procession? Above all, where is it leading us, the procession of educated men? . . . Let us never cease from thinking – what is this 'civilization' in which we find ourselves? What are these ceremonies and why should we take part in them? What are these professions and why should we make money out of them? Where, in short, is it leading us, the procession of the sons of educated men?

Such questioning has been twisted in times of sexist assertiveness into arguments for keeping women out of stringent formal education (see ch. 3). After all, why waste valuable laboratory facilities on girls who get married and waste it all?

The phalanx of professional women born with the century filled the teaching posts created by educational expansion, quietly consolidating the hard-won opportunities forged by the suffragettes. These were the women who taught us in the 1950s, who shaped our lives and our minds and whom – God forgive us – we pitied for their spinsterhood. Retreat into private life and domestic virtue, the predictable pattern after many a previous and subsequent holocaust, was impossible for those whose marriageable mates were wiped out in the trenches. (We pay tribute to those who taught us and who still teach and love us, their surrogate daughters.)

Even the established church made sleepy but hopeful overtures about the admission of women to its professional ranks. It was not until 1935 that the Church of England admitted that the deaconness order it had created for women was an alternative rather than a precursor to full priesthood. Women ordained before 1935, some of whom are still in the fight for whole priesthood, remind the church today that they are indeed in holy orders, ordained to a now broken promise.

By the late 1930s, less than 150 years after its founding, the women's movement, arguably the foremost influence on our Western culture, was reduced and trivialized in official history texts to pastiche and parody. Female liveliness and rebellion were subsumed into media male wish-fulfilment images of boop-de-doo flappers lisping through cupid's bow lips, 'I'm a poor little rich girl, give me Fun, Fun, Fun!', or to blue-stockinged bespectacled brainboxes on bicycles needing only the unlikely but longed-for embrace of Mr Right to crush them into dizzy delight. Those bloomered leftovers from pre-war days who had chained themselves to railings joined the ranks of Bertie Wooster's funny aunts – 'such a rum old bird'. Test this observation by counting the number of pages, probably paragraphs, devoted to the women's movement in children's history books. Check the descriptions of Virginia Woolf on paperback blurbs – scarcely a mention of her feminist commitment. In his excellent essay 'The Hard and the Soft', Theodore Roszak wryly comments that such omissions are probably caused by male historians being under-sexed.[21] The 1930s to 1950s did not witness daughters following in the footsteps of their preaching and lecturing mothers and grandmothers; they tended to enjoy the fruits of their parents' hard-won reforms. Thus for a time these older role models were lost, for our generation to rediscover.

The balance is being redressed today with a wide spectrum of feminist publications showing the scope of feminist activity in the first half of this century. The movement was neither élitist, nor its work remotely condescending, as is often assumed in images of 'do-gooding' ladies. The post-World War I era had made women acutely conscious of the need for practical solutions to women's social problems. Enter Marie Stopes and her American contemporary Margaret Sanger, who carried on the battle for effective birth control. In 1921, Marie Stopes opened Britain's first birth control clinic, a statement making her efforts sound beguilingly simple: backlash against family planning was predictably strong in the church. Countless opponents derided her as a perpetrator of pornography and a greater threat to civilization than Hitler.

Women's history in the twentieth century cannot be understood without describing the toll taken by World War I, the Depression and the rise of Fascism in Europe. Military and political vengefulness, manifested in the Treaty of Versailles (1918), left the defeated German empire without hope or dignity. The war preceding the humiliation of peace thus became the legend inspiring bloodstained fantasies, providing a balm for unmentionable frustrations – at least for the man later to turn the aftermath of World War I into the major cause of the second, to create the most hideously masculine ideology of the twentieth century. Hitler thanked heaven that he'd been alive during those 'halcyon' days of the Great War. (More recently, we hear that the nuclear warlords of our era use the term 'Wargasm' to speak the possibility of global annihilation.)[22]

Voices of sanity from within the church during the 1930s and 1940s (Dick Sheppard of the Peace Pledge Union, Bishop George Bell) inevitably saw that efforts for peace were not given a chance. In the later stages of the war Bell denounced the indiscriminate bombing of a nearly defeated people. Such voices were largely lone and reviled.

We leave to students of social history the detailed documentation of women's silence from the beginning of the 1930s through the 1940s and 1950s until our 'second wave' of feminism. A generalized but tantalizing observation will perhaps suffice: *when optimism about human possibilities becomes secondary to survival itself, women, on whom sheer biological continuance depends, opt out of history.* This basic realization needs to be incorporated into

the more widely recognized radical ideal summed up in the following words of Charles Fourier written in 1841; it needs to be drawn
on positively in socialist doctrine!

> The change in a historical epoch can always be determined by
> the progress of women towards freedom, because in the relation
> of woman to man, of the weak to the strong, the victory of
> human nature over brutality is most evident. The degree of
> emancipation of women is the natural measure of general
> emancipation.[23]

Simone de Beauvoir did not opt out of history. In 1949, uncowed
by the Nazi holocaust from which the Western world was still
reeling, she wrote *The Second Sex*.[24] Sphinxlike she rests in our
minds, resolute, determined to state her case on her own terms.
She argued that the quarrel over feminism was essentially over,
that the time had come for clarity and understanding. With eclectic
skill, she drew from the disciplines of history, literature, biology,
anthropology and sociology at a time when specialization was the
acceptable mode of scholarship. She equated human progress with
the progressive 'masculinization' of history, maintaining that the
devaluation of traditional femininity was a necessary step in evolution. The victory of reason over superstition, of method over
magic, meant that the emancipated woman should be a taker; she
must refuse the passivity that men would impose on her. She must
work and create on the same terms with men. She must join men
in the *Angst* of work in the world and cease to be bribed into
enjoying immunity from the risks that men traditionally take.

Thirty years later, from our perspective of wanting *everything*,
we can see that our collective health will not necessarily be improved by homemakers exchanging their frilly pinnies for business
suits. Or, as Roszak says: 'How shall this already brutish and
bastardly world be saved by increasing the number of brutes and
bastards among us?'[25] Nonetheless, a reading of *The Second Sex*
made us angry with society and the power it gave to men to
determine and define women's possibilities. Looking back, one can
see that de Beauvoir's major contribution was in her fusing of
economic and reproductive explanations for women's subordination. She cleared our minds if she did not nourish our spirits;
the book did not generate widespread feminist awareness when it
was published, nor did it stimulate any political activity. Although
de Beauvoir rightly gives this book pride of place in her collected

works, she has wondered herself what *The Second Sex* would have evolved into had she waited another ten years to write it.[26]

The withdrawal of women into private life after the horrors of the 1930s and 1940s was but half of a universal story. The endeavours of the Second World War, brave though they were in defeating Nazism, ended in that ultimate act of cynicism – Hiroshima. The carnage produced a deep-seated revulsion in radical and conservative alike, although conservatives were more likely to offset and disguise dismay and shame by military glorification and talk of 'necessity'. Thoughtful men and women were deeply wounded and turned inward to the world of the home to rediscover workable human values. The world of the 'rat race' (a term coined in the 1950s which sums up ambivalence and distrust of public projects) was made morally unattractive to women when jobs were hard to come by and were felt to be the preserve of the returning heroes. The return of prosperity served to harden the pattern.

In other words, home became for men as well as women the place where real life happened and women were encouraged by every possible device to make the haven work and build the new Jerusalem in suburbia. Human hope built on such a timid premise was bound to fail. We witness that failure today in the negatives of divorce statistics, especially after the mid-1960s, and the positives of a resurgence of feminist consciousness which bravely but alarmingly asserts that it will all have to get worse before it gets better.

Betty Friedan's book *The Feminine Mystique*, described as the book that 'started it all', was published in 1963. The story of woman's return to kitchen and nursery is told with its accompanying rationale exposed and its wider political expediency revealed. Housewifery expands to fill the time now available; home sewing and home-baked bread are a playing pre-industrial revolution game as a hedge against meaninglessness. Women's forming a flexible cheap labour pool becomes but one way of supporting dubious economic policies. (When labour is scarce, women are encouraged into the labour force; when it is plentiful they are forced out and back on to the pedestal.)[27]

Nearly twenty years after its publication, *The Feminine Mystique* is seen to have picked up for a popular audience the themes explored by de Beauvoir: women should see the domestic myth for what it is and get back to work. Friedan's seemingly parochial brief was to study the housewifely discontent lurking behind the gingham-curtained windows of middle America. She chronicled masses of medical evidence of hysteria, from vast dependence on tranquillizers to mysterious psychically-related illnesses.[28] Women had bought a role image – the Happy Housewife Heroine – and Friedan traced the inception and perpetration of the image through the changing nature of women's fiction and film star ideal, from the gutsy good sport to the adorable dumb dolly. Friedan urged women to shed a pernicious role and restore the balance of private and public in their own lives, both in and for the lives of their children and their country. The severity of the problem, Friedan pointed out, had been exacerbated by post-war prosperity, which had made it possible for the first time in history for such a wide range of humankind to afford to sustain such an élitist and waste-making fantasy of the Good Life. (We discuss in ch. 3 the price exacted in human sexual spontaneity.)

Friedan's assessment describes religion in negatives, as a barrier to progress towards self-realization: 'Women of orthodox Catholic or Jewish origin do not easily break through the housewife image; it is enshrined in the canons of their religion, in the assumptions of their own and their husbands' childhoods, and in their churches' dogmatic definitions of marriage and motherhood.'[29] She goes on to describe the additional pressures on religious women to conform: sophisticated psychiatric techniques are summoned to the aid of age-old clerical prohibition to reinforce the mystique and keep women in their rightful place.

More recent polemic has been somewhat dismissive of Friedan's work, especially of her blinkered emphasis on the cream of middle-class motherhood which, for some, has masked the universality of her message; society is wasting half its assets – Wollstonecraft's ghost again. In her published diary of post-*Mystique* activities, Betty Friedan recalls a meeting with Simone de Beauvoir.[30] This essay created for us an atmosphere of bizarre non-communication. We pictured Betty Friedan, the well-groomed middle-aged cheerleader face to face with the inscrutable sphinx with all the pain and courage of the eternal Resistance etched on her face. Nonetheless, Friedan's book was an important step in our personal journey towards understanding the mechanisms that hold women in thrall. Perhaps only a Betty Friedan, with all the accoutrements of Mrs America, could effectively call the bluff of the fat married look, the warm and well-lit ivory tower of chosenness and togetherness; the sheer smuggery of complacent prosperity. When Mrs America herself explodes the myth (how different from our own First Lady!), something is happening. Women inhabiting the bastions of security that Friedan describes might easily dismiss the more profane polemic of Betty Friedan's descendent sisters, but her attack was direct and polite enough to demand a response.

In this highly personalized synopsis, we are now in danger of losing what little distance we have. The feminist thinking of our own time is so prolific, its insights and demands so unprecedented and daunting, that they are beyond the scope of this chapter and indeed this book. The messages that our minds have encompassed and assented to permeate the remainder of our text. The reader will be shaping his or her own responses and personal history and may, we hope, recognize ours.

The decades are catching up with our own lives. A growing peace and civil rights movement was the backdrop of our awakening political and religious consciousness. Harsh political experience in the early 1960s was to transmute the crusade into the New Left. Traditional political, religious, cultural and sexual mores disintegrated in an explosion of rebellion and protest. Radical Christians really did expect some new life to emerge from the theological ferment of the mid-1960s, whose widely-recognized milestone was the publication of Bishop John Robinson's book *Honest to God*.[31] Robinson restated the theological content of sexual and political questions. For a while it seemed that a theological reflection of contemporary uncertainties was widely heard and welcomed.[32] Women especially were bound to be disappointed yet again on both secular and ecclesiastical fronts.

The present women's movement evolved from the honest but persistently squashed longing to be part of history and of making things happen, rather than acting as history's safety valve and victim. Some of the boys we grew up with, marched and campaigned with, still wanted old-fashioned menial mothering and furthermore expected 'hip' sexual servicing, minus, of course, the traditional cushioning of personal commitment. Who were we, comrades or chicks?[33]

Germaine Greer, in *The Female Eunuch*, pinpointed the next step. The personal is political. Old-style feminists like Friedan and de Beauvoir were misleading women as they exhorted them to transcend rather than transform their sexual relationships – a stance, Greer maintained, that was damaging to women's sexuality itself. The greatest obstacle facing women is their own inability to love *themselves*, rendering them impotent to challenge definition and circumscription. Part of Greer's thesis and today's consciousness is that the conservatives may have been right all the time.

Society as it is has much to fear from women's liberation, but human survival itself demands that we bravely forge entirely new patterns of human relationships.

The Christian church purports to be the vehicle for asking and assessing questions of ultimate value and guards as its central treasure a concrete vision of a 'new deal'. But the church is debilitated by its all-too-human propensity to hang on to tradition in response to voracious human demand for change and liberation. Still reeling from the onslaughts of rationalism in all its forms, the church is simultaneously confused by higher criticism from within – by de-mythology, re-mythology and a general bombardment of '-isms'. Bloody but unbowed, the church is still here, insofar as it remains a symbolic echo of all our woes and joys. It will do well (for it really does not have the choice) to continue surviving the shaking of its foundations by looking at the women's movement. If the church fails at this last fence, the endurance required for all the others may have been in vain.

For women's condition can only be truly understood – and here we grope for language that does not exist – when the church itself examines all levels of its traditional complexity, beginning with the timeless models inherited in its scriptures.

2

Daughters of Eve

'God then formed Lilith, the first woman, just as he had formed Adam, except that he used filth and sediment instead of pure dust . . . Adam and Lilith never found peace together; for when he wished to lie with her, she took offence at the recumbent posture he demanded. "Why must I lie beneath you?" she asked. "I also was made from dust and am therefore your equal." Because Adam tried to compel her obedience by force, Lilith, in a rage, uttered the magic name of God, rose into the air and left him' (Midrash, as retold in Graves' *Hebrew Myths*).

'So, in studying and testing a people, or a period, by the question, "How did they treat their weak?" we must allow the collective word to include the women with the lunatics, the very poor, the mentally or physically infirm' (Norah Lofts, *Women in the Old Testament: Twenty Psychological Portraits*).

*   *   *

Bible stories are the earliest stories we remember. They drifted into our young consciousness, clustered around moments of blinding joy like Christmas, weaving themselves into a universally shared childlike curiosity about how we and our world came to be. Later, when we were schoolgirls, stories of other gods and men were poured into our minds, peopled other new and strange lands for us: we learned, for example, of another strange mythic biological reversal, the birth of Pallas Athene, who is said to have erupted full-grown from the head of her father Zeus. However much this more mind-bending (literally!) nativity of woman may have the edge on all that Genesis narrative about spare ribs and bitter fruits, we have to acknowledge as Christians that our most vital journey of discovery of the world that men have made and described is the biblical one. Our own quest for a mature woman's respect for and

understanding of the books which constitute the Bible is scored
with pain and anger.

We began years ago with some very naïve questions. Judging
from experience in teaching in Sunday School these questions do
not seem to have changed much. It is appropriate at the outset to
underline a basic truth: biblical enquiry leads us to the very well-
springs of human enterprise – it leads us to explore, because the
Bible in true mythic fashion *moulds the way our culture perceives
and organizes reality.*

Any brief contemplation of human history will in some measure
reveal the resistance of ecclesiastical authorities to the impact of
many great liberation moments and movements of human history.
This resistance has consistently involved invoking the Bible as a
statement of 'finished' and static divine truth. The Holy Bible has
been used to prohibit and discredit the work of such men as
Galileo, Copernicus, Darwin and Freud. It has been invoked
against projects for human liberation: the Abolition movement,
numerous struggles for racial and economic equality, and of course
the long struggle of women for social and spiritual recognition (the
vantage point and inspiration for this book). A deeper understanding through biblical study of the culture in which the Bible was
written, and the most cursory knowledge of *how* it was written
will teach the student that (s)he cannot turn this wellspring of the
human/divine experience into a rule book. History teaches that
human perceptions of truth are never 'finished', nor can God be
imprisoned in the pages of a book or the walls of a church.

At what point in our own lives did it become personally unacceptable that the protectors of Holy Writ and even the Book of
Books itself left out the stories of its women? Any feminist who
takes on a serious biblical study has to pass through a kind of
spiritual endurance test in order to acquire a spiritual second wind
before she can recover any of the childhood fondness she once felt
about the stories, before she can respect the text, to find that a
measure of love and truth remain. Personal blinkers of avoidance
and romanticization have to be reckoned with. The psychic map
of the past seemed to look different every time we took it out, but
a transition from love and confidence to a sense of depression and
betrayal *did* occur. Like a fatally flawed marriage, the unacceptable
and irreconcilable warts emerged in spite of considerable efforts to
deny their existence.

Perhaps the following Bible story will provide an example of
what we mean by 'spiritual endurance test'. The story is found in

chapters 19–21 of the book of Judges. A certain Levite's concubine
has run away from her husband to return to her father's home in
Judah. The owner/husband goes to the father's home, and pleads
with his concubine to return to him. The narrative implies that the
girl's father was extremely glad to see the Levite. No doubt his
daughter's unexpected return had imposed burdens of one kind or
another. She must have agreed after several days to return to her
husband/owner, and on the way back to the Levite's home in
Ephraim, the couple stopped for the night in Gibeah, a village of
the tribe of Benjamin, where they were offered hospitality by an
old man. The story continues:

> As they were making their hearts merry, behold, the men of the
> city, base fellows, beset the house round about, beating on the
> door; and they said to the old man, the master of the house,
> 'Bring out the man who came into your house, that we may
> know him' [i.e. have sex with him]. And the man, the master of
> the house, went out to them, and said to them, 'No, my brethren,
> do not act so wickedly; seeing that this man has come into my
> house, do not do this vile thing. Behold, here are my virgin
> daughter and his [the Levite guest's] concubine; let me bring
> them out now. Ravish them and do with them what seems good
> to you; but against this man do not do so vile a thing.'[1] But the
> men would not listen to him. So the man [the Levite] seized his
> concubine, and put her out to them; and they knew her, and
> abused her all night until the morning.

At daybreak, the young girl, mortally ravaged, stumbles to the
threshold of the host's door and collapses. Her master urges her to
get up and set off on their way. When there is no response (evi-
dently she is already dead, but the narrator does not say), the man
takes her body home, hacks her into twelve pieces and summons
the other tribes to wage battle against the Benjaminites by distrib-
uting bits of the girl's body throughout the territory of Israel. When
the tribal council gather, the Levite gives a pathetic and outraged
version of the tale. The result was a war which according to the
narrator well-nigh obliterated the tribe of Benjamin.

'Objective' biblical scholarship points out that this narrative is
really about tribal conflict, national identity and the laws of hospitality. After all, anyone with a grain of understanding knows
that the Bible is not for the faint-hearted. There are many instances
in the Old Testament where women have been thrown to the mob;

but men have suffered a similar fate, too, in the pages of Holy Writ. Commentaries describe the incident:

> The laws of hospitality here . . . *obviously* took precedence over consideration of *chivalry* towards the female sex (italics ours).[2]

> The wickedness of Gibeah is aggravated by the fact that it was perpetrated against a *man* who was both a Levite and a sojourner (italics ours).[3]

Another shows a bit more sympathy (under the sub-heading: 'The War between Israel and Benjamin'):

> The Levite's anger does not arise out of compassion for his abused concubine, for whom he seems to show no personal concern, but out of the feeling that *his own dignity* and *property rights* have been *violated* (italics ours).[4]

If, for a moment, we remove our 'objective' spectacles, if for a moment we begin to ask 'why?', then we are dealing with another kettle of kosher. In our personal case, a naîveté about what we thought scripture *should* do clashed with what we discovered when we actually read it. We had thought, for example, that the Hebrew claim to chosenness as God's people involved a rejection of human sacrifice and a valuing of human life. We realize that the narrator was not justifying the grisly and tragic treatment of the concubine, but we found ourselves asking: What set of social circumstances made it possible to consider females as expendable as boiling fowls? What brutality committed by the feared and abhorred pagan Canaanite cults could have been worse than this? How did this particular version of history come about? Why did she run away from her owner/husband? Why is she not named?

These observations are not original. Nearly a century ago Elizabeth Cady Stanton, an ardent and prominent American abolitionist (see ch. 1) and suffragette, said:

> There are many instances in the Old Testament where women have been thrown to the mob, like a bone to dogs, to pacify their [men's] passions; and women suffer today from these lessons of contempt, taught in a book so revered by the people.[5]

Late in life Elizabeth embarked on a mammoth task. She gathered a group of women biblical scholars together with the intention of publishing a woman's Bible. The brief of the group was to address itself to women's visible oppression by exploring their biblical invisibility. She is probably the first feminist theologian. She explained her reasons for undertaking this huge project in her autobiography:

> I had long heard so many conflicting opinions about the Bible . . . some saying that it taught women's emancipation and some her subjection . . . the thought came to me that it would be well to collect every biblical reference to women in one small compact volume and see on which side the balance of influence really was. To this end I proposed to organize a committee of competent women, with some Latin, Greek and Hebrew scholars of the Old and New Testaments, and to ascertain what the status of women really was under the Jewish and Christian religion. As the Church has thus far interpreted the Bible as teaching women's subjection, and none of the revisions by learned ecclesiastics have thrown any new light on the questions, it seemed to me pre-eminently proper and timely for women themselves to review the book. As they are now studying theology in many institutions of learning, asking to be ordained as preachers, elders, deacons and to be admitted as delegates to Synods and General Assemblies, and are refused on Bible grounds, it seemed to me high time for women to consider those scriptural arguments and authorities.[6]

Mrs Stanton and her colleagues sought to write a thorough commentary on the Bible through examining both its narratives and blatant exclusions of women. The completed work took six years to write, and was published in 1895 when Mrs Stanton was eighty years old. In effect *The Woman's Bible* was a kind of women's *Talmud*.[7] The real curse of womanhood, imply the commentaries, is not so much the intentional cruelties perpetrated by men upon women, but the hidden premise that permeates every thought and action of both actor and acted upon in the biblical drama: that man is rightfully dominant and naturally entitled to the prerogatives attendant thereto. This underlying assumption affects every aspect of life. Elizabeth Cady Stanton was conscious of this pervasive blindness, of its subtleties and of its absurdity. *The Woman's Bible* was repudiated in Mrs Stanton's own lifetime, and would have doubtless disappeared completely were it not for the dedication of this last decade's feminist scholarship. Disappearance has also been the fate (to our knowledge) of the one translation of the Bible by a woman, Julia Smith, a contemporary of Mrs Stanton. Without assistance, she completed five translations

of the Bible from Greek, Latin and Hebrew.[8] It is not our purpose
here to review Mrs Stanton's book. Much of it is quaint, peculiar
and out of date. To our knowledge it is no longer in print. But its
existence points out that feminist biblical scholarship is no new
thing, and that contemporary perspectives on biblical studies have
an honourable precedent. It is interesting to recall that a good
many of Mrs Stanton's own contemporaries and companions in
the secular struggles that chiefly occupied her energies exhorted
her to stop flogging the dead horse of biblical tradition, recognize
its irrelevance and get on with the pressing tasks of the present
day.[9] This admonition has about it a ring of ghostly familiarity one
hundred years later!

What has subsequent feminist scholarship unearthed in its patient and thorough examination of scripture? Furthermore, how
can women begin to weave themselves once again into the spiritual
fabric of religious tradition? With these questions in mind we begin
our own woman's journey through the Bible, and dedicate our
efforts to the memory of Elizabeth Cady Stanton.

(a) Old Testament

The context of Israel's history is set in the book of Genesis, and
the second (and fuller) of the creation accounts makes clear at the
outset the subservience in the created order of female to male. The
Genesis account of paradise lost also makes clear that Eve bears
prime responsibility for yielding to the temptation of the beguiling
serpent: 'The woman whom thou gavest to be with me (your fault,
Yahweh), she gave me fruit of the tree (her fault), and I ate (naturally!)' (Gen. 3.12). Even the serpent does not escape female association and is linked in Jewish legend with Lilith, who tries to
destroy the innocent bliss of the garden by becoming a barren,
bitter, shriek owl-like creature whose greatest pleasure is to threat-
en the sanctity of family life and steal babies. It is perhaps
unnecessary here to restate the extent to which this myth
undergirds our thinking to this day ... 'Hell hath no fury like a
woman scorned', etc.

Discrimination against women was inherent in the religious and
socio-political organization of Israel from its earliest written
records. The legal features of the Pentateuch: slavery, concubinage,
polygyny, the extended family, patriarchy, served to institutionalize
a double standard which seemed beyond anyone's right to question.
The biblical focus of legal questions is mainly on external threats

to a male's authority, honour and property; often the laws serve
to define a man's rights in relation to other members of his own
household.[10] For example, if a master struck his male or female
slave, and the slave's death resulted from the blow, the master
could receive an unspecified punishment. If, however, the slave
happened to survive the blow 'for a day or two', the master was
not to be punished, 'for the slave is his money' (Ex. 21.20f.).

A disobedient child could be punished with death: were he found
persistently rebellious, the parents could go to the elders of the city
who would decide whether he should be stoned by the male members
of the community (Deut. 21.18–21). Regarding wives the law
is also clear in its protection of a man's interests and authority.
There is an almost capricious tone to the opening lines of
Num. 5.11–13, called the 'law of jealousy', and the only example
of trial by ordeal in the Hebrew scriptures: ... 'if the spirit of
jealousy come upon him [the husband] ...' A husband's suspicion
was reason enough to subject the wife to a bizarre and frightening
test of wifely virtue. Whether she passed the test or failed it, the
passage informs us that 'The man shall be free from iniquity, but
the woman shall bear her iniquity' (v. 31).

Laws concerning adultery were brutal, too. The punishments for
adultery ranked with murder, and demanded death for both of-
fenders (Lev. 20.10f.). However, infidelity by a husband was not
considered a criminal act unless the partner was wife to another
man. Polygyny was a concession to the male desire for more than
one sexual partner, and in the broader sense a way of ensuring
rapid population growth.

Biblical scholars are generally agreed the texts which deal with
conditions and provisions for divorce are written later than the
main body of Hebrew legal writings. Divorce is written into the
law as an exclusively male prerogative. Barrenness was probably
the chief grounds for divorce, although concubinage was a common
solution to male marital discontent. The grounds for divorce in
Israel are unclear; sexual infidelity is indicated in the story of Hosea
and Gomer. Other prophets often use the divorce of a man from
an unfaithful wife as a metaphor for God's 'divorce' from an
unfaithful Israel. No abstract legal prescriptions dealing with divorce have survived. The following vague account is the only ju-
dicial statement on divorce in the entire Old Testament:

> When a man takes a wife and marries her, if then she finds no
> favour in his eyes because he has found some indecency in her,

and he writes her a bill of divorce and puts it in her hand and sends her out of his house, and she departs out of his house, and if she goes and becomes another man's wife, and the latter husband dislikes her and writes her a bill of divorce and puts it in her hand and sends her out of his house, or if the latter husband dies . . . then her former husband, who sent her away, may not take her again to be his wife, after she has been defiled [and presuming that she has not committed suicide by this point!]; for that is an abomination before the Lord, and you shall not bring guilt upon the land which the Lord your God gives you for an inheritance (Deut. 24.1–4).

We know from I Samuel 25.44 that there is precedent for a father's stepping in to terminate his daughter's previously arranged marriage.

Widows in Israel had no economic or legal security beyond the nebulous Levirate marriage practice. Widows were classed with aliens and orphans, and were denied any participation in cultic, legal or economic life because they lacked identification or function within the family. A widow was regularly reclassified (echoes of South Africa) as 'resident alien' (Deut. 14.29). Levitical scripture left widows and orphans to God's care. The prophets later took up the cry of the oppressed, but before that time the best these groups had access to were the 'gleanings' of society. The subject of the 'single woman' is not discussed anywhere in the Old Testament. They were non-existent or invisible.

Laws concerning uncleanness and impurities are extensive and fascinating in their method of categorization. Briefly, the laws that affected both sexes were concerned with defining and legislating over states of 'impurity' – leprosy, skin eruptions, contact with a corpse, bodily emissions of all sorts, regular and irregular. Many laws made a good deal of sense in the simple, often harsh, living conditions of an early nomadic community – scorching heat, scarcity of water. However, even a cursory study of the laws affecting women, in particular, reveals that these circumscriptions go beyond hygiene into the realm of asserting female subservience and inferiority. During child-bearing years particularly, women were almost totally excluded from cultic participation by virtue of their natural biological rhythms. Menstruation certainly 'cramped their style' for several days each month. In addition to an arbitrary period of seven days' untouchability, her neighbours and loved ones would be unclean if they came in contact with anything she touched for one day after the contact, and if she were to have intercourse, the man would carry her uncleanness with himself for seven days (Lev. 15.19–24).

Most fecund females were probably pregnant during a significant portion of the child-bearing years. The ritual for 'cleansing' after childbirth was rigid: on the birth of a male child uncleanness lasted for seven days with circumcision on the eighth day; after another thirty-three days the mother was seen as 'clean'. Were she to bear a female child, the period of 'purification' was twice as long – fourteen days of untouchability, sixty-six days when entry into the sanctuary was forbidden to her (Lev. 12.1–5).

This dreary catalogue of restrictions inhibiting women's participation in the public cult did indeed perpetuate a man's religion. There were no women priests in Israel. The feminine form of the word 'priest' does not appear in the Old Testament. The 'magic' of priesthood (handling the holy things in the sanctuary) and the 'magic' of childbirth appear integrally related concepts of male and female roles in Levitical law. The Israelites believed that Yahweh opened wombs and allowed birth to women. Barrenness was a shame and reproach in Israel. When at last Abraham's wife Sarah conceived and bore a son she said, 'God has taken away my reproach' (Gen. 30.23).

> When Rachel saw that she bore Jacob no children, she envied her sister; and she said to Jacob, 'Give me children or I shall die.' Jacob's anger was kindled against Rachel, and he said, 'Am I in the place of God, who has withheld from you the fruit of your womb?' (Gen. 30.1f.).

The legends of the patriarchs' wives – Abraham's wife Sarah, Isaac's wife Rebecca, and Jacob's wife Rachel, all three of whom were barren – illustrate the importance of Yahweh's participation in the continuing of the covenant. Thus for a woman to be barren was to be bereft of Yahweh's pleasure and approval, and of status in her own community.

Rare laws protect the rights of dependants. There were protections for a young woman swept away by Israelites as booty after battle (remember all those Cecil B. DeMille multi-million-dollar extravaganzas featuring gorgeous nubile scarlet-lipped girls?). She was to be bathed, scrubbed, allowed a month to mourn her lost homeland; then (and no one asks her permission) she must marry her captor. He is given full legal sanction to throw her out if he 'have no delight in her'. A concession to her is that her captor is forbidden to sell her as a slave (Deut. 21.10–14). Women under socially-sanctioned polygamy were protected by a law against favouritism. The husband was enjoined to treat the sons of both loved and disliked wife equally; e.g., if the firstborn son were the offspring of the disliked spouse, the father must nevertheless honour him as the firstborn and give him his full entitlement (Deut. 21.15–17).

Under another compensatory law, a man could be whipped for falsely accusing his wife of not being a virgin at the time of their marriage.

> If any man takes a wife, and goes in to her, and then spurns her, and charges her with shameful conduct, and bring an evil name upon her, saying, 'I took this woman, and when I came near her, I did not find in her the tokens of her virginity,' then the father of the young woman and her mother shall take and bring out the tokens of her virginity to the elders of the city in the gate; and the father of the young woman shall say to the elders, 'I gave my daughter to this man to wife, and he spurns her; and lo, he has made shameful charges against her . . . And they shall spread the garment before the elders of the city. Then the elders of that city shall take the man and whip him; and they shall fine him a hundred shekels of silver, and give them to the *father of the young woman*, because he has brought an evil name upon a virgin of Israel . . . he may not put her away all his days (Deut. 22.13–19).

The ritual of parading a bride's bloodstained garment (a sign that the hymen was intact and penetration effected) is still practised today in parts of the Middle East; then, as now, the 'proof' was open to laughable exploitation, a dubious relief for the bride.

The punishment befalling the young woman should she be found guilty, is predictably grim:

> 'But if the thing is true, that the tokens of virginity were not found in the young woman, then they shall bring out the young woman to the door of her father's house, and the men of her city shall stone her to death with stones, because she has wrought folly in Israel by playing the harlot in her father's house; so you shall purge the evil from the midst of you (Deut. 22.20f.).

Female life, it seems, was very cheap, and stones handy.

The strictness and unevenness of punishment in the above law can be understood when one remembers that female persons were property; thus, as property devalued, a woman of this kind was a plague on both the houses of her father whom she deceived and her husband whom she misled.

There are exceptions to the general rule of women as legal non-persons; the woman was granted equal authority as a parent. Jewish scholars, and Jewish culture to this day, would maintain this sphere to be of paramount social and spiritual significance. Much of the book of Proverbs is devoted to describing the crucial role of parentage and the harmony of domestic life as holding vital importance for the 'good life'. The mainstream of Jewish scholarship would deny that this is compensatory discrimination.

Punishment for witchcraft was also meted equally to male and female: 'A man or a woman who is a medium or a wizard shall be put to death; they shall be stoned with stones, their blood shall be upon them' (Lev. 20.27). Cult prostitution was forbidden to man and woman alike (Deut. 23.17), as were acts of incest, buggery and bestiality (Lev. 20.10–21). 'Uncovering' someone's nakedness was a serious crime for both sexes. Outrage and infamy were a great leveller between the sexes.

The legal status of women in the Old Testament can be summed up in the following way: she is dependent all her life, first and ultimately on her father, and then on her husband when she marries. The laws by and large do not address her. Her importance is circumscribed by her childbearing function and the law ensures that the patriarchal context of that function is upheld.

In this climate it is perhaps surprising that some strong female personalities manage to surface in the historical, prophetic and poetic books of the Old Testament. (Women's stories occupy some ten per cent of the narrative.) Rarely but significantly women appear as prophets: Deborah (Judg. 4.4–16) was prophet and leader/judge in premonarchic times; and Huldah (II Kings 22.14–20) was a late monarchic prophet under King Josiah. Deborah is by far the better known and can be described as the 'token woman' of the Hebrew testament. She pops up with dreary regularity in any discussion where sexist bias or female invisibility is suggested. In fact, her prophetic role and her song (Judg. 5) are about militaristic strategy and triumphalism. She is no St Joan; the warrior Barak is the real hero of the piece.

Women like Esther and Ruth become significant in their own right (with their own books). They play a healing role in tribal stories of patriliny and military power. Jezebel and Delilah take the opposite role as 'baddies', temptresses, seducers. They achieve a colourful distinction, but the vast majority of Old Testament female characters are portrayed as types of womanhood. They are either idealized as super-mums, super-wives, super-queens – or vilified as temptresses, seductresses, deceivers, stupefiers, betrayers, sorcerers, in a plot whose story revolves around the deeds of men.

Some of the prophets saw beyond the present order. They looked for a new act of God in human history, to a new order with unforeseen possibilities for human existence. Amidst the often parochial and legalistic admonitions of the prophets, some far-sighted visions shine jewel-like:

> And it shall come to pass afterwards,
> that I will pour out my spirit on all flesh;
> your sons and your daughters shall prophesy;
> your old men shall dream dreams,
> and your young men shall see visions.
> Even upon the menservants and maidservants
> in those days, I will pour out my spirit (Joel 2.28f.).

> The wolf shall dwell with the lamb,
> and the leopard shall lie down with the kid,
> and the calf and the lion and the fatling together,
> and a little child shall lead them.
> The cow and the bear shall feed;
> their young shall lie down together;
> and the lion shall eat straw like the ox.
> The suckling child shall play over the hole of the asp,
> and the weaned child shall put his hand on the adder's den.
> They shall not hurt or destroy in all my holy mountain;
> for the earth shall be full of the knowledge of the Lord
> as the waters cover the sea (Isa. 11.6–9).

> How long will you waver,
> O faithless daughter?
> For the Lord has created a new thing on the earth;
> A woman protects a man (Jer. 31.22).

Many feminists would contend that we are now entering this era. If they are correct, now is a good, though frightening, time to be alive (see ch. 7).

(b) New Testament

The Christian religion grew out of the rich spiritual soil of Judaism. As it separated from the synagogue, it gained an independence from the myriad legal circumscriptions of Jewish faith and practice. Jesus himself transgressed Jewish law on several occasions. One notable example was when he healed a man of dropsy on the Sabbath. The scribes and Pharisees tried to catch him out and he answered them with plain good sense, confounding their criticisms (Luke 14.1–6), asserting that he had come not to destroy the law but to complete and fulfil it. Early Christianity also incorporated ideas from the diverse cultures present in the Hellenized Roman world, as well as in the mystery religions present in the Roman Empire at the time. The predominant flavour of the early church as captured for us in the writings of the New Testament – its egalitarianism, its pooling of resources and its victory over racism (as in Acts 11) – augured well for a victory over sexist bias. Jesus' revolutionary treatment of women is recorded by his biographers and conceded by even the most reactionary churchmen today. Women disciples were the first witnesses of Christ's resurrection (Luke 24.1f.); Christ's conversation with the Samaritan woman at the well broke down some very rigid social barriers (John 4.7–26); the Martha and Mary story demonstrates Jesus' appreciation of the ministry of women in a sphere other than domestic (Luke 10.38–42). For many Christian feminists, the story containing the most hopeful image of Jesus' love was the story of the woman with the issue of blood. In Christ's loving recognition of the woman's faith, he healed both her terrible affliction and the ritual uncleanness which accompanied it, a grand-slam blow against body hatred (or as Germaine Greer more ripely puts it, the 'cunt hatred' that is the hallmark of male supremacist society to this day). Feminists and non-feminists alike recognize the extent to which the ritual uncleanness of menstruation still subconsciously applies to women in our own culture. It is sometimes used as an argument against female priesthood.

While Gentiles, along with slaves and women, held no theological status under Levitical law in Israel, it appeared that in Christ the stage was set for a new order of creation. The account of the setting up of the first Christian communities recorded in the book of Acts chronicles this hopeful evolution towards 'commonism'. One by one the tin gods of classism, racial supremacy, and sexism (the 'ism' undergirding all the others) are exposed, and glimpses of their being disposed occur throughout. The women whose names are mentioned in Acts and in some of the epistles seem to have been educated, and they seem to have taken roles of leadership.[11] In spite of these glimpses, honest observation of the whole New Testament picture of women (and slaves) gives no actual liberation guidelines. Were one constrained to view the New Testament as a once-for-all textbook of social reform, there are ample texts to corroborate that as a result of the order of creation women and slaves are eternally subordinate. The Pauline injunctions summarized below provide the better-known passages on the domestic position of women. In Luther's *Catechism*, these commands are known as 'Haustafeln' or 'domestic lists'.

> 'Wives, be subject to your husbands, as to the Lord. For the husband is the head of the wife as Christ is the head of the church. . . Husbands, love your wives, as Christ loved the church and gave himself up for her. . . He who loves his wife loves himself. For no man hates his own flesh, but nourishes it and cherishes it. . . For this reason a man shall leave his father and mother and be joined to his wife, and the two shall become one' (Eph. 5.22–33).

Love and order are seen as male provinces, while obedience and submission are the province of women, children and slaves: 'Wives, be subject to your husbands . . . Husbands, love your wives and do not be harsh with them. Children obey your parents in everything, for this pleases the Lord . . . Slaves, obey in everything those who are your earthly masters . . .' (Col. 3.18–22). Older women are bidden to reinforce the above order: 'Bid the older women . . . to teach what is good, and so to train the young women to love their husbands and children, to be sensible, chaste, domestic, kind, and submissive to their husbands . . .' (Titus 2.3–5). One can see the beginnings of the tradition of the sober and godly matron in the following passage: 'Let not yours be the outward adorning with braiding of hair, decoration of gold, and wearing of robes, but let it be the hidden person of the heart with the imperishable jewel of a gentle and quiet spirit, which in God's sight is very precious . . .' (I Peter 3.3–5).

Theological utterances concerning women's behaviour in the assembly are less consistent. There were women preachers and prophets, and the office of deacon was open to men and to women. The office of priest does not belong to New Testament vocabulary, nor does the concept of the Trinity. It is yet a while before the priestly office of the Old Testament or of the Roman and Hellenistic worlds influenced the concept of priestly ministry in the Christian church. However, all other New Testament utterances on the position of women, save one, Gal. 3.26–28 (discussed later), take for granted their secondary status in the order of creation as dictated in Gen. 3.16: 'I will greatly multiply your pain in childbearing; in pain you shall bring forth children, yet your desire shall be for your husband, and he shall rule over you.'

In his early letters Paul was convinced that the 'last days' were upon the Christian community: he enjoined Christians not to change their life-styles; the unmarried were better off single because of the heavier earthly responsibilities of family life. He urged those already married to live celibate lives because . . . 'the appointed time has grown very short . . . For the form of this world is passing away' (I Cor. 7.25–31). These 'last days' exhortations are sometimes referred to as 'interim ethics'.

Paul's instructions to the church at Corinth to maintain traditional patterns are clear: 'But I want you to understand that the head of every man is Christ, the head of a woman is her husband, and the head of Christ is God' (I Cor. 11.3–16).[12] Paul was unequivocal in his advice to the church at Corinth concerning women in the assembly. Silence and subordination were the order of the day. Any questions a woman might have could be answered by her husband in the home, because . . . 'it is shameful for a woman to speak in church' (I Cor. 14.34f.).

By the time of the Pastoral Epistles the urgency about imminent judgment day had eased a bit, but the exhortations about women at worship remain stern. Women were urged to refrain from public pronouncement, on the basis of the order of creation, the argument used with the Corinthian church. Woman's salvation would derive from her ability to have babies and keep quiet: 'Yet woman will be saved through bearing children, if she continues in faith and love and holiness, with modesty' (I Tim. 2.11–15). Clearly concerned with order in the worshipping community, these letters are also arguing against the Gnostic 'libertines'[13] who were threatening the stability of the young church at that time. One purple passage condemning both seductive preachers and silly culpable women reveals how powerful the charisma of the 'treacherous deceivers' must have been: '. . . those who make their way into households and capture weak women . . . who will listen to anybody and can never arrive at a knowledge of the truth' (II Tim. 3.6f.).

Of the many fermenting ideas debated in the young churches,

the Gnostic 'heresy' most certainly had the greatest influence. One line of Gnostic thought maintained that by abolishing their roles as sexual beings and mothers, women could enter into equal partnership in redeemed humanity. The secret Gospel of Thomas contains a tantalizing conversation between Peter and Jesus. Peter suggested that Mary should be excluded from the disciples because she was a woman. Jesus replies, 'Behold, I shall lead her, that I may make her male, in order that she may also become a living spirit like you males. For every woman who makes herself male shall enter the kingdom of heaven' (Logion 114).[14]

The above passage diverges sharply from Paul's pyramidic pronouncements in the 'Haustafeln', and from his insistence that childbearing was woman's redemption. Recent studies of the Gnostic gospels indicate that two very different patterns of sexual attitudes emerged in orthodox and Gnostic circles, and that these differences may have influenced the excessive discrimination against women reflected in the orthodox canon. Elaine Pagels discussed the explosive social possibility that women, being thought by some gnostics to have derived from an androgynous deity, could act on an equal basis with men in positions of leadership.[15] This possibility might lead one to conclude that the gnostics were suppressed primarily because of their positive attitude towards women, albeit emerging from a male-centred concept of the self in which the female is neutralized through becoming male.

Whatever the exact nature of the Gnostic controversy, its Pauline countermandings were disastrous in their effects on the social and theological standing of women in Christian history. The biblically accepted view of the dualistic split between spirit and body perceives woman as inferior and somehow more prone to evil. Philo, a Hellenized Jewish contemporary of Paul's, reveals unwittingly how theology can distort human culture and progress:

> Now for the man there is a place where properly dwell the masculine thoughts – wise, sound, just, prudent, pious, filled with freedom and boldness, and akin to wisdom. And the women's quarters are a place where women's opinions go about and dwell being followers of the female sex. And this sex is irrational and akin to bestial passions, fear, sorrow, pleasure and desire from which ensue incurable weaknesses and indescribable diseases.[16]

This misogyny is depressing for women. But Paul had great virtues, too, and some of his sideswipes at the Gnostics have become memorable as the most powerful passages in the New Testament. His hymn to love, for example: 'knowledge puffs up, but love builds up' (I Cor. 13). A letter to Timothy prophetically warns of the disastrous effects of dualistic thinking – the apostasy that the church experienced in so much of the thinking of the early fathers:

> Now the Spirit expressly says that in later times some will depart from the faith by giving heed to deceitful spirits and doctrines of demons, through the pretensions of liars whose consciences are seared, who forbid marriage and enjoin abstinence from foods which God created to be received with thanksgiving by those who believe and know the truth. For everything created by God is good, and nothing is to be rejected if it is received with thanksgiving; for then it is consecrated by the word of God and prayer (I Tim. 4.1–5).

Paul's letter to the church at Galatia has been called the 'Magna Carta of Christian Liberty'.[17] Paul insists that people become right with God through faith in Christ and not by performing good works and ritual observances, or by passing through the requirements of the Mosaic law before becoming Christian. The Mosaic Code, Paul explained, was keeper of the sacred until faith should be revealed, a sort of caretaker until Christ's culminative life: 'For as many of you as were baptized into Christ have put on Christ. There is neither Jew nor Greek, there is neither slave nor free, there is neither male nor female, for you are all one in Christ Jesus' (Gal. 3.23–28). So the consequence of baptism is to be in Christ, and to be in Christ is to transcend the Law of Moses in the following areas: (*a*) the boundary between Jew and Greek is abolished – no more racist supremacy; (*b*) the boundary between slave and free is abolished – no more classist supremacy; (*c*) the boundary between male and female is abolished – no more sexist supremacy.

This passage is in tension with the Levitical order of creation and breaks through the rules of the Haustafeln. In his excellent pamphlet *The Bible and the Role of Women*, Krister Stendahl says: 'In Christ the dichotomy is overcome; through baptism a new unity is created, and that is not only a matter discerned by the eyes of faith but one that manifests itself in the social dimensions of the church.'[18] Christian feminists are often criticized for giving such weighty emphasis to a passage in what is after all a very short Pauline letter, one admittedly at variance with other teachings.

There are other virtues to Galatians. The book boasts the wonderful 'fruits of the spirit' passage (5.22f.), as well as the best sign-off line in all of Paul's writing: 'Henceforth, let no man trouble me; for I bear on my body the marks of Jesus' (6.17). It is therefore small wonder that women attach such hope to the Galatians passage. It offers a glimpse of human liberation in Christ which reaches far beyond the game of first century 'bibliolatry', and brings women completely into the continuing drama of God's working through the centuries which have passed since the Bible was written. Until now the old dualistic model has 'worked', either in the crude and heretical form expounded by Philo, or in the anthropological bedrock assumptions of biblical patriarchy itself, i.e.: man = endeavour, initiative, bearing in stewardship the destiny of mankind on his frail shoulders, naming and controlling the natural world; woman = fatalism, passivity, uncontrollable mystery, bearing in her body and psyche the anarchy and danger of the natural world.

Our own generation is called to find spiritual meaning and salvation in the midst of a series of revolutionary changes that have rendered the old model not only untrue but unworkable. A view of scripture is at stake. How do we and how *should* we read the Bible? The present day church will have to overcome its sexist schizophrenia: 'Is it not a kind of spiritual schizophrenia to say, as the apologists for legalistic interpretation of the New Testament would insist, that there is a difference between equality before God and equality before society? Is the person who justifies slavery and racism with biblical texts to be taken seriously today?'[19] Women have as vital a part to play in the kingdom as men; if they were to be defined, blessed and saved through their biology, through childbearing alone or through subservience to men, then God's world would quickly come to an end, through over-population if nothing else!

As a history of religious consciousness the Bible traces in its narratives and its silences the secondary status of women. Our woman's journey through the Bible opened old wounds which are still healing. More importantly, though, it has taught us the relevance at the heart of this great book of God's people. We shall continue to read it, to study it, without watering it down or falsifying, without jettisoning it in favour of something with more immediate appeal. Perhaps most importantly we will learn from its silences not to absent ourselves from history. By entering into history, women may become part of the quest for the truth that lies beyond history. To be in Christ is then truly to be part of an entirely new mode of human existence.

3

Daughters and Lovers

'Shun immorality. Every other sin which a man commits is outside the body; but the immoral man sins against his own body' (I Corinthians 6.18).

'The absence of respect for women's lives is written into the heart of male theological doctrine, into the structure of the patriarchal family, and into the very language of patriarchal ethics.' (Adrienne Rich, *Of Woman Born*).

'I did not know there were seven deadly sins; please tell me the names of the other six' (A young man to Dorothy L. Sayers).

*　　*　　*

The jubilation expressed by euphoric crowds of Iranians when the Ayatollah Khomeni was restored to them was, in part, an expression of the people's weariness with Western values, values they felt had eroded their national life for far too long. The strength of feeling against the dubious benefits of American capitalist involvement was accompanied by a deeper rejection of Western sex-soaked decadence. A number of Iranian women graduates even took proudly to the purdah again with a profound sense of relief. The Ayatollah purports to re-assert traditional Islamic values with a renewed fundamentalist fervour, using when necessary the force that theocracy brings in its wake.

We in the prosperous West are rightly fearful of government by religion; such distrust is, in fact, built into the American constitution. Experience of witch hunts in New England, the earlier Inquisition in Europe and present-day crusades against contraception by less enlightened sections of the Catholic church teach us that government by God as King produces more heat than light in times of political turmoil. However, in the areas of sexual behaviour and inter-personal relationships, Christians in society have been suffering the awesome uncertainty of shedding really new light on old ethical values. Neither fear nor heavy-handed moralizing, especially that of a weak and alienated church, can ever restore men and women to all that is true and tender in traditional values.

No loving person would deny that the image of Woman-in-Purdah and the image of Woman-in-*Playboy*-magazine are distortions of human sexual love and longing. Both are signs of violent action and reaction. We need to look at the turbulent changes of our time and discover which of these have imprisoned us; to describe what we see as an ethical vacuum. For us, the insights of feminist thought make an immense contribution.

Human sexual behaviour and the relationship between men and women have been altered by far-reaching biological, social and economic factors. Birth control; smaller families as a possibility and even a necessity; longer life and therefore longer marriage accompanied by changing patterns of financial and domestic inter-dependence, have all affected our approach to marriage – widening its possibilities while simultaneously threatening its permanence. Without doubt, the church has a vested interest in marriage and is expected somehow to enhance and uphold the institution – a dubious burden shared with political leaders seeking election. Conventional wisdom in the church assumes a suspicion of (*a*) sexual experimentation before marriage, creating a climate for (*b*) casual and impermanent relationships, thus leading to (*c*) open attitudes to marriage itself, leading to (*d*) the social chaos of widespread 'easy' divorce. This domino theory of permissive sex, with its consequences of instability and suffering for adults and more especially for their children, is no less rigid or unclear than theories by exponents of permissiveness who, in recommending (*a*), deny any connection between (*a*) and the following.

Any one of the above practices carried dire consequences for both women and the existing social order until this century. The vital realities of a woman's life made permanent male protection a primary aim. Her life was shorter, with more children, few educational hopes and almost no professional opportunities. Efficient means of birth-control were not widely developed until the nineteen-twenties and were at first slow to reach those whose overburdened lives most needed it. Contraception remains to this day unavailable to those in greatest need either because it is physically or financially inaccessible or because implementation presupposes a degree of autonomy and planning that many women find an impossibility. Venereal disease was an omnipresent danger to life and health until brought under some degree of control with the advent of antibiotics.

Family stability traditionally serves as a protection for the interests of women and children. But it is also a vital component of the patriarchal culture and free-enterprise economy that necessitates such protection. Both wifely fidelity and fertility are essential to the man who accumulates wealth to pass on to his (male) children. To the poor man parenthood represents the deeper needs of the psyche for personal immortality. In either case, failure to comply with either of the two wifely necessities can result in death or divorce for women all over the world. Strict control over wives, jealousy and the penalties inflicted for unfaithfulness and disobedience have roots, not in helpless love but in notions of ownership. Women have, in the past, made a virtue of necessity and taken pride in the protective jealousy of their mates as a sign of personal/market value. However, mutually appeased vanity has by no means assured a mutuality of vision, and feminists would claim the above rather hard-boiled reductionist view necessary to examine and expose the ubiquity of the double-standard, for such exposure is a first requirement in any examination of sexual ethics that is worthy of respect. In contemporary Western culture, the control of women's lives by men is being eroded by rapid social change and by the accompanying changes in our psyche brought about by women's liberation. The extent and rapidity of such change can be observed in the reversed expectations of those who opposed the liberalizing of divorce law in the mid and late 1960s. In the event, the provisions of the 1967 Act were extensively used by women to initiate release from long-dead marriages, overshadowing fears of a 'Casanova's charter'.[1]

The teachings of the Christian church have always upheld monogamy and chastity as values in themselves, both for doing God's will and for grace and meaning in our lives. This spiritual vested interest has led many to mourn the passing of social systems which support Christian teaching as necessity. Monica Furlong, writing in 1965 at the other end of the present sexual revolution, describes 'the sort of Christians who believe that Christianity is a device for stopping VD and for shoring up family life against the inroads of divorce and lust' as beset by a 'finger-in-the-dyke complex'. Miss Furlong urges an equally precarious but more creative exercise: 'In the effort to learn more about loving, Christians need to mop up secular insights with shameless greed.'[2]

Well, fifteen years later, we've mopped up a good few, willingly or grudgingly. Feminist thought has unwittingly joined Christian caution in questioning the benefits of present permissiveness. We have begun to see that the old protections to women must be replaced rather than shed to strengthen women in their quest for bodily sovereignty. A useful example of this realization can be seen in the recent women's movement campaign against sexist exploitation in advertising and entertainment. When women descended, armed with stickers and tins of spray paint, to declare THIS DE-GRADES WOMEN on underground posters, they risked arrest. When women walked the streets of Soho to 'Reclaim the Night' in protest against the even more degrading exploitation of women in the shadowy world of 'live' shows and strip clubs, they risked the violence and hatred of women that London night-life projects. In either case the female crusaders were portrayed by the media as unattractive harridans, unable to compete in either meat or marriage market, or the poster plethora of Pretty-Polly legs and sensually lingeried ladies. The media stereotype of beauty undoubtedly damages. It damages those who measure up to it as much as those whose frail flesh fails the myth of the eternal feminine. In either case, for Christians, no image of prized flesh can ever measure up to that given us by that biblical whipping boy of feminist critique: 'Do you not know that your body is a temple of the Holy Spirit within you, which you have from God? You are not your own; you were bought with a price. So glorify God in your body' (I Cor. 6.19).

Even the miraculous pill has its sinister side. While appearing to be a passport to liberated sexuality and female autonomy, it is psychically seen by many as a ticket to permanently available women and disposable relationships. It is all the more dangerous to women because it has brought with it a chimera of enlightenment.

We are both now thirty-eight. As we left our twenties, early in the last decade, we were both closely involved in the life of a predominantly young, largely student community. As such, we were friends and counsellors to many young women living out the familiar dramas of love and work. The chronological generation gap – about ten years at most – was exaggerated by a disparity of experience, caused partly by our own early commitment to marriage and motherhood. Retelling our own experiences to younger women forced us to confront the reasons for our own behaviour light years ago in the early 1960s! We had grown up in a climate which insulated us from sexual adventures. In recalling the advice

of the mothers who largely inspired us we could begin to understand that all three generations were prisoners of their decades as
well as the century itself. In the prevailing social and sexual climate,
backed up by mothers' warnings and reinforced by the advice of
surrogate parents – teachers, tutors and landladies – our adherence
to conventional morality was common. We were free to resist
sexual encounter without loss of face. We could not, in all honesty,
have separated our convictions about chastity from the rewards
that went with it: a 'good name', immunity from the psychic and
physical risks of full sexual expression. The teachings of Christianity were but a shadowy background, a distant confirmation that
there were changeless rules in a breathless world.

The dilemmas facing our post-pill sisters ten years on made us
grateful for this protection as we contemplated the waste of spirit
and joy in so many unwanted and unneeded sexual relationships.
To be sure, the compulsions we laboured under had altered by the
early 1970s, but spontaneity still seemed to be shackled by the
dead hand of man-made rules. The word 'permissiveness' itself has
a passive and negative ring. Who permits whom to do what?
Exponents of 'free love' in our day taunted us with accusations of
'trading sex for security', but such had been the way of the world
for generations, and somewhat easier to counter than the deeply
personal sneers of 'frigid', 'screwed up' or 'neurotic' levelled at
women today. How easy it is to begin thinking like those sweet
old ladies who bemoan the passing of Romance. 'We knew a thing
or two,' they say with a wink. A brief contemplation of the economic protect-and-survive significance of granny's ankle-flashing
disperses any vestigial nostalgia. Rather, it is in the dual disillu-
sionment of both the over-romanticized versions of sex we were
brought up with and the subsequent recognition that the sexual
revolution was more sexual than revolutionary, that the seeds of
sisterhood were sown for our generation.

Mother's generation, unsustained by the changeless certainties
that had died with World War One, was nonetheless unable to
agonize over the same questions we did. They did not ask if it was
'all-right-to-do-it-if-you-were-really-in-love' or if 'going all the
way' was more or less hypocritical than 'heavy petting'. Those
doom-laden euphemisms, surviving today in such grim phrases as
'settling down' to describe marital commitment, recognized that
there was indeed no second chance for love's young dream when
our mums were young. Fear and necessity in those pre-pill days
had a large part to play in making good girls good; doing the 'right

thing' by a girl 'in trouble' has shackled many an unwilling young couple. Daring experimenters were either superhumanly careful or the women long ruined or married. Only the very rich could find ways and means of escape. Even so, divorce and abortion were matters of dark notoriety.

The early 1960s, 'our young day', was a period in which the complacency and conservatism of the 1950s had, in its death throes, sought to impose its claims to immutability in our own young lives. So widespread had been the retreat from higher education and the professions back to the home that many pundits of the day thought education for women was pointless when it was bound to be wasted. This was the central theme of Sir John Newsome's famous report, published in 1964 and defended in these terms:

> The influence of women is exerted primarily in their role as wives and mothers, to say nothing of aunts and grandmothers. Even in employment outside the home, with the exception of schools and hospitals, this influence usually works by sustaining or inspiring the male. The most superficial knowledge of the way in which the affairs of government, industry and commerce are conducted makes this quite plain. What infuriates a rather esoteric group of women is that they want to exercise power both through men and also in their own right, and this is almost impossible.[3]

Countering such ludicrous dogmatism was an important early step towards feminist consciousness. We had come up to university to change the world, even if we were somewhat naïve about its sexual politics. In the drama of 'the new woman' we were determined that some leading roles had to be severely cut or written out of the script altogether. The Newsome woman was the first to go, using educational opportunities to secure a better qualified meal-ticket. The next starring role to be killed off by the scriptwriters was 'the ruined maid'; or as she was called in the not-so-realism of the fifties, 'second-hand goods'. Christian doctrine and mythology are guilty of encapsulating the ideal of chastity into a crude and technical concept of virginity. For women, genital sex has been a kind of Rubicon, river of no return. One slip and lost for ever, one rosebud and that's your lot, meant that a girl could be declared a prostitute and unmarriageable. In some societies this still holds true. We wondered, listening to mother's warnings, how men could sow their necessary wild oats and yet want a chaste, virginal bride.

Nobody knew, yet it was darkly whispered that it *was* so and so
we believed it. Not today; the play is closer to live theatre than
erstwhile domestic comedy and tragedy, and the dialogue is certainly more lively. This is a tribute to both actors and setting.
Certainly it is an enormous step forward for the privileged who
can take advantage of the miraculous side of the sinister pill.

By the end of the 1960s, a new set of choices seemed to be
clearly emerging for women – opportunities to embrace the fullness
of professional, intellectual as well as personal discovery. Heady
stuff! So we had been right in our student days; there was something brewing.

The rhetoric of the Roman Catholic Church against scientific
contraception is an attempt to enforce, in the lives of both privileged and poor, the connection between sexual activity and pro-
creation. The result of the church's sanctions is bondage for those
who cannot or will not resist them and alienation and derision
from those who do and can. Worse still, the distinctions between
the life-enhancing possibilities of planned parenthood and the sad
consequences to mothers and babies brought about by abortion
are all smothered in a judgmental blanket of 'not-getting-away-
with-it'.

A far cry from St Paul's thrilling and frightening imagery describing the cosmic and eternal significance of our sexual behaviour. Deeper than fertility lies the meaning of love-making. We are
joined, we become one flesh. The implications of this are light
years from the weary myth of 'Sex as Fun', equally distant from
the sanctions of a loveless church in its attempts to tie women to
their bodies for fear they will lose their precarious souls. Among
the troubled love stories of our time we find that serious artists are
concerned with exposing Fun-Sex as the mirage it is. Bertolucci's
dark and frightening film *Last Tango in Paris* is a powerful evocation of the destructiveness of loveless gratification. In Erica Jong's
Fear of Flying, her heroine's quest for the 'zipless fuck' is doomed
to failure.[4] Both works have achieved a notoriety that masks the
seriousness of their statements. Even at the heights of joy that
sexual love can bring, we only begin to grasp Paul's teaching about
God's gift to us. Christianity, even at its most distorted and dualistic, recognizes human sexuality as a source of spiritual experience.
Though it was feared and shunned by the Fathers, they knew its
power, if only in negatives. Celibacy vaunted as a way to holiness
was an attempt to short-circuit the currents of love and to give to
God the creative energy otherwise deflected by love in the flesh.

If religion can be a substitute for sex, a godless culture needs to look to its woes and ask whether sexuality has become a substitute for religion. Betty Friedan clarified and demolished Fun-Sex's twin heresy: 'Sex explains all'.

We are living through a period in which a great many of the higher human needs are reduced to, or seen as, symbolic workings-out of the sexual need. A number of advanced thinkers now seriously question such 'explanations by reduction'. While every kind of sexual symbolism and emotional pathology can be found by those who explore, with this aim, the works and early life of a Shakespeare, a da Vinci, a Lincoln, an Einstein, a Freud, or a Tolstoy, these reductions do not explain the work that lived beyond the man, the unique creation that was his, and not that of a man suffering a similar pathology. But the sexual symbol is easier to see than sex itself as a symbol. If woman's needs are not recognized by herself or others in our culture, she is forced to seek identity and self-esteem in the only channels open to her: the pursuit of sexual fulfilment, motherhood, and the possession of material things. And, chained to these pursuits, she is stunted at a lower level of living, blocked from the realization of her higher human needs.[5]

In the reductionist deification of human orgiastic experience (or the implications of lacking it), the mysteries of potency and orgasm are studied with zealous and technological precision. How St Paul would have laughed at the notion of having sex on the brain!

Whatever the current golden calves of our sexual religion, the price of idolatry is paid in the lives of women. What does Christian vision offer now to heal the wounds partly caused by its own distortions in the mouths of men? Any discussion of sexuality and the chaos wrought by a new search for meaning needs to recognize, but not be limited by, history. To assuage collective guilt, we are tempted to fall over backwards in showing how broad-minded we are and how lovely all this new freedom is. But we can only begin to discern God's purposes by meeting people in the midst of their pain, by creating opportunities for encounter and sharing. Places where such encounter is apparent, the Rape Crisis Centres and Women's Aid refuges, for example, are the results not of lofty idealism or less lofty concepts of 'unfortunate women' but of feminists' practical and imaginative response to violation and helplessness. The church neither founded these organizations nor often sends its followers in a similar direction.

Where has the church gone wrong in making its teachings loving
and credible? Paul is the major moralist of a church that has largely
concentrated on the restrictive and legalistic side of his teachings.
Both Paul and his followers have insufficiently heeded a Hebrew
sense of the indivisibility of body, mind and spirit. Christian truth
responds essentially to human longing for love and goodness. Tragically, this longing has been answered not by gospel but by law.
The hungry people look for visions of wholeness and are handed
a rule-book. Modern feminist assertion is creating a new forum for
the fundamentalism debate in its critique of patriarchal legalism.
'What we see,' says Adrienne Rich, 'is the one system which recorded history has never actually challenged, and which has been
so universal as to seem a law of nature . . . the power of the fathers
has been difficult to grasp because it permeates everything, even
the language in which we try to describe it.' [6]

Our Christian obligation is to describe the distortions of Jesus'
gospel message in the language it had come to transcend. The most
powerful word that Christian tradition can tentatively claim is the
word 'forgiveness'. Because 'forgiveness' is, to a degree, a ghetto
word, its central meaning has not become so diffused as that of
the ultimate word 'love'. 'Love' can be used to describe a multitude
of experiences from red-hot reifying lust to simple apple-pie nice
warm feelings. Forgiveness, though, has about it a squirmy uncomfortable ring. Few will say that they never love, but many will say
that they will not or cannot forgive and even expect to be praised
for their strength of feeling. Forgiveness is always joined in the
gospels to that other uncomfortable word 'sin'. It is the possibility
of forgiveness which enables us to face our own sins and the sins
of others head-on. A church that has allowed its sacred ideals of
monogamy and chastity to be wielded as tools for male supremacy
and female repression needs not only to preach forgiveness to
sinners; it has itself to be forgiven as an institution. A forgiven
church is still entrusted with a healing mission to transform and
redeem relationships. Its very forgiveness is, for the church and its
people of every age, the key to humility – the humility with which
to address the sin of the world. ('Humility' is even more of a ghetto
word than 'forgiveness'; a good many people don't even think it
is a good idea.)

A popular baptismal hymn (English Hymnal 337) contains the
line:

'In token that thou shalt not flinch

Christ's quarrel to maintain. . .'

The belligerent language is initially shocking. Christ's quarrel? Where ought Christians to have a quarrel with the world, or in relation to the present subject, with the more negative demands of the Women's Liberation Movement? Feminist thought, as we understand it, is concerned both with defining areas of oppression and creating structures for growth and justice. But there is an arena of doctrinaire and tyrannical rejection of the male-structured world which many feminists, Christian and non-Christian alike, see as a mirror image of an all-too-familiar history. It is difficult to talk about the group within the women's movement who represent the unacceptable face of feminism without seeming to agree with a world that labels them man-hating viragos.[7]

'Radical feminists' is probably the best word, since it is a self-chosen name. These women, in totally scorning male approval and protection, feel themselves able to give the only disinterested critique of society. Many radical feminists are politically, if not practically, lesbian. The more extremist fringe of the present movement is spearheaded by a new separatist caste of lesbian sisters. (A sad example of this sexual apartheid appeared in *Spare Rib*'s classified section: 'URGENT: we need space for a creche in the Albany St/ Regents Park area, London NW1, as the Women's Arts Alliance want to stop admitting boy children to the premises. If you can help, etc . . .')[8] (Updated in preface to second edition, p. xvi.)

Radical feminists would define the religious significance of sexual behaviour, what Christians call the holiness of human sexuality, as nothing more than the working out of a historical oppression against women. Monogamy and the nuclear family are seen solely as instruments of patriarchal power, without hope of redemption. Christian feminists are unfailingly aware of the reasons for these responses, but nonetheless see a transcendent quality in human sexuality – how could they fail to, when it is the fabric of eternity and incarnation? Many of us remain involved in the day-to-day life of the church because, at whatever level of consciousness we would defy patriarchal power, we believe in the redemption of the church and its flawed sexual imagery as tools for the liberation of God's people. Eleanor McLaughlin and Rosemary Radford Ruether defended such loyalty thus:

Feminists today are apt to be especially attracted to rejected groups – heretics and even witches – expecting to find among them subversive views expressing feminist rejection of patriarchal religion. But in our opinion much of this search is mistaken. It is difficult in any period ... for persons to remain sane and mature from a stance of radical rejection of and by the normative culture. Important women do appear in marginal movements, but they are not more important than women leaders who arise at the centre ... Orthodox theology is appropriated by such women with a radicality and depth of insight that transforms it into an expression of the full personhood of women.[9]

Orthodoxy is most profoundly threatened, not by the ritual or invective of the separatists, but when they actually claim the normative culture through the traditional role of motherhood. Technological sophistication has made it possible for women to conceive babies by artificial insemination, totally bypassing male ascendancy over their bodies and their children. This denial of fleshly fatherhood as a means and source of joy seems to many like us more a bitter revenge than a creative alternative. 'Am I a king or a breeding bull?', reputedly asked Henry VIII. The answer is probably 'yes' to both, and the pathos of his statement is hollow, coming from one who killed his wives and whose whims blighted the lives of his children. We do not approve of old Henry. He did not handle power at all well. But we would contend that the dismantling of the Kingdom of the Fathers surely means the restoration of *fleshly* fatherhood to its rightful place rather than its obliteration. Men, too, need the human hope of children, unalloyed by dynastic imperatives. Millennia of women as cows and sex-objects will not be redeemed by men as studs or bulls.

The more radical impulses to female separatist power are an inevitable part of a movement's growing pains. The women's movement is, nonetheless, sufficiently broad-based to contain checks and balances in the form of critique arising from within. We count ourselves among the critics. Because we see an unacceptable face, we are in honour bound to distinguish between female separatist attempts to claim the normative culture and an age-old male separatist ethic which not only claims culture but is the author of it.

Such distinctions are important in a response to the demands of present-day male homosexuals for recognition. Gay men justly and rightly articulate their need for love and acceptance to a church and world that has ghettoed and shunned them, and the resulting debate is an important one. Christian distortion and ambivalence are dramatically pinpointed in the plight of the homosexual. Some of our own deepest love relationships are with gay men. Happiness and ease in their company goes deeper than a misplaced vanity that we are both somehow 'safe' with each other. Feminists who share and affirm a need for love uncircumscribed by patriarchally enforced patterns are often those most hurt by the fear and disdain of women that the male gay subculture frequently projects. (This alienation is not peculiar to questions of homosexuality, but can be observed in the rich ferment of many latter twentieth-century liberation movements, as we have shown in chapter 1.)

The church in this country is seriously attending the voices of Gay Liberation. The Gay Christian movement, especially, is teaching the church to reflect on that part it has played in creating the erstwhile twilight and fearful world of the homosexual.[10]

Public and ecclesiastical debate on this question seems to centre on the rights and wrongs of physical expression. In the church, Christians discuss the possibility of gay marriage blessed and celebrated by the church. Opinion and recommendation vary enormously. Some Christians struggle with ambiguous and thorny passages of scripture in Leviticus and Romans, some generalize the dilemmas by re-examining Pauline teaching that genital sex is for heterosexual monogamous marriage only. Some even agonize over the story of Sodom. Evidence of increasing homosexuality has led some traditionalists to kill two liberationist birds with one stone and lay the problem at the feet of uppity women, whose increasing belligerence has made the role of family headship decidedly less attractive! Most of the world, of course, waits with what Monica Furlong describes as 'less than bated breath' upon the present spate of church deliberations. What is extraordinary to us, though, is that nowhere in the published material is there any deep examination of the formative influence that the male-dominated structures of the church may have exerted and may continue to exert on homosexual preferences and behaviour.

Reticence to discuss the 'causes' of homosexuality is understandable: we personally find it difficult to discuss our own convictions about homosexuality and Christian distortion because discussion of causes so often lapses into crypto-medical and psychiatric jargon, which seems to us dangerously near to speaking of homosexual preference as an illness. That is the old view that hurt and maimed. Furthermore, so much conventional psychiatric wisdom is dedicated to adjusting individuals to 'proper' societal roles, a task woefully unenlightened without a psychopathology of society itself.[11] What we do know, however, is that many men in our culture receive much of their formative experience and education in exclusively male-peopled and male-governed institutions, and that these patterns of sexual apartheid were largely set by the church in the days when it held sway over these matters. Those in the church and the world who hold up their hands in horror at homosexual behaviour are those least likely to demand the change of what many in society would baldly term 'breeding grounds'.

Sexual apartheid in the church is spiritually enshrined in the religious life itself. Since the Reformation, which restored marriage to a degree of dignity, the church has tended to extremes in its treatment of celibates; has made them into a holy and superior caste or, in Lutheran tradition, deemed them unnatural. Clearly, celibate vocation, rooted in bodily and psychic reality or embraced in a spirit of loving sacrifice, should be recognized and retained for the enrichment of all. But the tradition has its shadow side, has been both haven and apologia for its own particular brand of homosexual (in the sense of one sex) ethic. This is not to confuse celibacy with homosexuality (though many do – 'must be something a bit odd about them'), but to assert that the tradition of the monks and the fathers is *spiritually* homosexual. Their long-preserved power can justly be described as ecclesiastical homosexuality. The virulent misogyny of much patristic thought and teaching (discussed in chapters 5 and 6) leads us today to question the distinction between gay power and gay love in the context of organized religion. We felt that this tension was clearly visible in the 1978 General Synod debate on women's ordination, when arguments from tradition were forcefully urged to exclude women from the priesthood. So the question remains and must be answered: Where does tradition inform a hatred of women? Furthermore, how much does hatred of women inform some male homosexual preferences among those in the church? Those in positions of power in the church have a special responsibility to seek an answer. One of our correspondents wrote thus after the 1978 Synod . . . 'homosexuality, *in itself neutral*, but not when linked to a hatred of women and a wish to justify the homosexual by hints of uncleanness in women'.[12]

In this context, an increasing demand for the right to express homosexual love physically from the clergy themselves can be seen as a sinister compounding of spiritual and material power; a use of permissiveness to stratify structures in a physical and thus even more pervasive way.[13]

Where two claims to power – the power of the fathers and the power of the mothers – undoubtedly clash is on the issue of abortion. We make no apology for grasping this nettle, for the implications affect the interests not only of those who can otherwise sit quite lightly, through personal harmony and self-realization, to the turmoils we describe here but of the next generation, and of those in society whose impulse to radicalism is rooted in the whole problem of private and public violence.

Abortion is seen by the vast majority of feminists as an important battleground of female autonomy. Even without this idealism, abortion is widely and openly considered by most women faced with an unwanted pregnancy. Many feminists, Christian and non-Christian alike, are dismayed at so much feminist energy being taken up with the negatives of female sexuality and fertility. Nevertheless, they question the motives of control and punishment in those who at present uphold the 'right-to-life' argument, which all too often sounds hypocritical in the mouth of a church which has, for most of its history, managed to co-exist with war, genocide and other death-dealing enterprises in the name of Holy Crusade or defence of democracy. If the right-to-lifers had their way, and if the argument were implemented and absolutized, then there could quite clearly be no abortion on ethical grounds. But then the world would be unrecognizable, as would the landscape of the present debate. There could be no space for the dangerously judgmental ambiguities implicit in the present practices: abortions could not be 'granted' or withheld as punishment or reward for more or less morally impeccable reasons (like rape or severe foetal handicap). We believe, though, that a world free from institutionalized violence and state murder would be one in which female autonomy and liberation would be dramatically closer to realization. In such a world, we would not be in the ambivalent position of asserting *agape* and absolutes in a public culture in which women bear most of the burden of respect for life; where medical advance in the field of contraception has placed the burden, with its life and death choices, firmly back on their shoulders.[14]

Those who urge the sanctity of the life of an unborn child rarely question the mother's responsibility for its nurture. Anti-abortion publicity rarely presents the adoption alternative as a creative choice. We simply see pictures of the 'good girls' who kept their babies – doing, of course, no more than their duty. A desperate woman, unable to make the fifteen- to twenty-year commitment, knows only too well that nobody else will do it for her.

To depict a woman's need for an abortion in our present society as a form of irresponsible refusal to 'meet her fate' (and this we believe is the dominant moral tone of such organizations as LIFE and the Society for the Protection of the Unborn Child) is as obscene as to regard free abortion on demand as a final triumph for female wholeness and freedom.

Let us be clear. Abortion is a tragic necessity.[15] To name it otherwise is dangerously to distort the creative potential of human sexuality. We must never forget that love and fulfilment can sometimes come with ill-timed or unwelcome babies; even with babies who are not whole and perfect. Denial of the reality that the unborn was not simply foetal material but an unborn *child* carries frightening *Brave New World* dehumanizing implications. In 1945, the black American poet Gwendolyn Brooks spoke profoundly in her poem *The Mother*:

Abortions will not let you forget.
You remember the children you got and did not get,
The small damp pulps with a little or with no hair;
The singers and workers that never handled the air.
You will never neglect or beat
Them, or silence or buy with a sweet.
You will never wind up the sucking thumb
Or scuttle off ghosts that come.
You will never leave them, controlling your luscious sigh,
Return for a snack of them, with gobbling mother-eye.
I have heard in the voices of the wind the voices of
My dim killed children.
I have contracted, I have eased
My dim dears at the breasts they could never suck.
I have said, Sweets, if I sinned, If I seized
Your luck
And your lives from your unfinished reach,
If I stole your birth and your names,
Your straight baby tears and your games,
Your stilted or your lovely loves, your tumults, your marriage, aches and your deaths,
If I poisoned the beginning of your breaths,
Believe that even in my deliberateness I was not deliberate.
Though why should I whine,
Whine that the crime was other than mine?
Since anyhow you are dead.
Or rather or instead

You were never made.
But that, too, I am afraid
Is faulty. Oh, what shall I say, how is the truth to be said?
You were born, you had body, you died.
It's just that you never giggled or planned or cried.
Believe me, I loved you all.
Believe me, I knew you, though faintly, and I loved, I loved you
All.[16]

This poem is both a mourning and a recognition. There is deep sadness and remorse but, more importantly, there is love and a turning away from despair.[17]

At the heart of some extreme feminist struggle there *is* despair – the kind focussed in the political struggle to reclaim women's bodies. Such despair would visit present oppression on the unborn. To cease to love our children, born or unborn, is to abandon a vital truth of our lives. The history of human struggle against oppression traditionally contains the hope of a better world for our children. But when our fertility itself is seen to be our oppressor, rather than society's violent and unjust exploitation of that fertility, then we are at an ideological impasse that only the reassertion of that theological virtue 'hope' can resolve.[18]

Committed Christians in the women's movement would hold this hope to be an inseparable part of Christian forgiveness and would withstand accusations from their sisters of going soft on the enemy!

The issue of abortion is one of many sexual issues that remain unresolved, explosive and fraught with complexity. Nerve endings are exposed and raw, as they also are in the gentler and more domestic debates, such as marriage and remarriage, that we discuss elsewhere in this book. There, too, as in this chapter, we assert that feminist alternatives to the contemporary confusion we attempt to describe are concerned with bringing all human love back into the fullness of its potential, not merely by dismantling the rules but by dismantling the power structures that make legalism so loveless. If the power of eroticism is to be harnessed in the service of the Kingdom of God, not that of the political mothers or fathers, it cannot be imprisoned either in rules or in wishy-washy permissive anarchy.

As pacifists, we deplore violence at the heart of the family *and* in the wider world. To this degree we are anti-abortion and to this degree our dream of a world where men, women and little children have reclaimed their value is as yet unrealized. But to lose hope is unthinkable.

4

Sisters of the Spirit

'. . . the Word within
The world and for the world;
And the light shone in darkness and
Against the Word the unstilled world still whirled
About the centre of the silent Word'
(T. S. Eliot, *Ash Wednesday*).

'Oh my God, if I could wholly love thee
Wholly be mine own, then I would not be snared
in loving all these fragments of thee'
(Robin Morgan, *The City of God*).

*　　*　　*

Feminist theology enjoins Western Judaeo-Christian theology to look closely and critically at the limitations imposed by its past, and challenges the heretofore exclusively male perspective of our history. Feminist students of Judaeo-Christianity are examining the whole of the Western religious tradition to discover how sexism has infected and distorted it. The judgment of these scholars is harsh. So far, traditional scholarship has not responded significantly to the challenges of this examination. We searched diligently, but were unable to discover any traditional opponents to the women's movement in the church who were actually conversant with the questions raised by feminist theologians.[1]

There is a considerable body of feminist biblical scholarship, though we would assert at the outset that Christian feminists are rarely fundamentalist in their approach to the Bible, and all would shun the snare of looking at biblical texts through legalistic eyes. Feminist vision and exploration propose, many believe, a new view of the Bible. In crystallizing our own ambivalent response to biblical texts, we found that the imagery of birth, so prevalent in biblical poetry, was the most helpful image we could use. Scriptures

inform and nourish our Christian experience, so we began to envisage the Bible not so much as a receptacle for all eternal truth
but as a kind of spiritual placenta. Not for one moment can the
importance of the placenta in early life be forgotten; but what
woman, what mother, would ever mistake afterbirth for newborn?
Biblical debate has so often been dedicated to finding reasons for
not nourishing and bringing forth life by acting in society. Reten-
tion of capital punishment, slavery, religious war, witch hunt and
antisemitism have all been justified by a selective use of scripture.
To use the Bible and tradition (read 'placenta') as a substitute for
the individual and collective experience (read 'baby') is to mistake
the unquenchable nature of the gifts these writers left for our
inheritance. All metaphor breaks down eventually, and we do not
intend to consign *our* placenta to the slop buckets of history,
though many of *us* need to concentrate on the fragile new baby
for a while.

Another generation of women may well be able to read the Old
Testament without pain. For us, the stories are so overwhelmingly
emptied of female insight that we are left with little other than an
impression of our own invisibility (see chapter 2). Some scholars
prefer finding new insight through the symbols and stories of other
traditions to looking long and hard into one's own misshapen
tradition for meaning. Nevertheless, the impressive range and volume of feminist biblical scholarship of the accepted canon gives
the lie to any impression that Christian feminists are merely dismissive of the Bible.[2]

The same holds true of our approach to history. We do attempt
to paint clear, broad-canvassed pictures, and in stripping some old
masters we expose some pretty bloody scenes and garish colours
that were best left covered with respectful age. We cannot afford
the luxury of some art historians in steeping ourselves in our own
beloved and jealously guarded periods or styles. Rosemary Radford
Ruether states:

> I do not apologise for a certain generality. Women's studies is
> addressing itself to a different task from that which has shaped
> traditional scholarship. For this reason all criteria of scholarship
> must also be different. First of all this is because the women's
> movement must encompass a far larger history than other move-
> ments. Liberation movements begin at the point of the subju-
> gation of their people ... the subjugation of women begins in
> pre-historic culture. The women's story must encompass the

entire scope of the human dilemma. Women cannot confine themselves to short sections of time or separation of fields, which give established scholarship its illusion of total mastery of its subject. To be sure, very specific studies, limited in time and field are needed. But even these studies must presuppose the comprehensive setting of the issue.[3]

Traditional interpretation of patristic theology has not yet found a way of clearly and succinctly acknowledging its undeniable misogyny while simultaneously discovering its timeless truths. This failure, along with feminist outrage, is probably increasing the likelihood that future lively theologians will give up searching for the nuggets and seal off the mine altogether. We are not asking traditionalists to reiterate endless reproaches, and we do believe there are undiscovered seams in the patristic mine, but we *are* offended with the benign indulgence of many traditional scholars towards the more virulent woman-hating passages. These cannot be softened by saying, 'Ah, but they were different times', those men *made* the culture of their age (or by saying that Augustine loved his mother!).

Feminist theology takes serious note of both scripture and tradition, and has indeed contributed to a clarification of the biblical and traditional elements in Christian practice. To take the example of priesthood, we find that some of the best respected theologians have (disingenuously?) given very muddled guidance. It is impossible to read most opposition cases without discerning some confusion between scripture and tradition. 'Our Lord' and 'the primitive church' are often lumped together in a way that implies that priesthood is a New Testament concept. From here and from the fact that Jesus *did* speak with respect of his own levitical tradition, it is quite easy to stir Old Testament and New Testament together with tradition and come out with a men-only recipe.

Setting the record straight about the seriousness of our biblical and traditional understanding is a simple matter – our credentials are there for anyone to read. We must attempt, as our central task, to measure the degree to which traditional concepts tremble at some premises of feminist theology.

Early in the 1960s, C. S. Lewis saw clearly that the pressure for women's ordination was building up and that the whole myth of 'separate but equal' was breaking down. He realized that fresh assertion of the spiritual equality of the sexes would involve a long hard look at sexual symbolism. He wrote:

Now it is surely the case, that if all these supposals were ever carried into effect, we should be embarked on a different religion. Goddesses [nobody had mentioned them then] have of course been worshipped, many religions have had priestesses. But they are religions quite different in character from Christianity.[4]

Lewis seems to be equating feminization with paganization. This kind of xenophobia has led many women to believe that their contribution to Christian insight is suspect. Lewis' statement was portentous in that it described a direction that women have in fact taken in their despair and fatigue over trying to participate authentically in Christian tradition. A few have turned to ancient goddess traditions, redesigning them to suit what are seen as specifically feminine needs – the exclusive role of the mothers as the flip side of the exclusive role of the fathers again. A Roman Catholic feminist wrote to us: 'I am somewhat disturbed by another trend in the women's movement – the harking back to a supposedly golden matriarchal age. I feel it is dangerous and the point is missed concerning our dilemma. Surely it is the *archal* aspect that is damaging – not who runs it?'[5] It is both damaging and unjust to Christian feminists to equate their yearning and questioning with a wish to depart from Christ's church. In their search for healing, the growing body of Christian feminists are asking some searching questions, but the questioning is neither iconoclastic *nor* over-protective of the church as an institution. Shoring up monolithic lies about women will not help the church to survive; it may indeed threaten the survival of Christian truth itself.

Lewis' not-so-subtle hints of paganism have precedents in the old dualism of sacred and secular; the view that says that we must not allow the political to encroach on the sacred, ancient hallowed timelessness of church tradition. Although such a view has lost respect in other fields, it is not slow to rear its head in the present debate, where it consigns the insights of Christian feminism to transient sociological trends and ephemeral fashion – presumably easily evaporated by changing one's newspaper and refraining from television chat shows. In 1972, Eric Mascall wrote a tract on women and priesthood; he relied heavily on this argument to present his opposition case: 'The church may be found to have committed itself to a course of action that future generations will condemn as reflecting the ephemeral and unsubstantial prejudices of the latter part of the twentieth century.' Feminist demand, in

Mascall's argument, becomes mysteriously connected to other uncontrollable forces of our century which have become our masters
instead of our servants: 'Far from presenting the appearance of a
social order which has discovered how to control and direct the
tremendous forces which science and technology have released, it
bears all the marks of a situation which has got thoroughly out of
hand.'[6]

How on earth did the abolitionists get away with it? Future
generations might (and probably did) regret such an irrevocable
step instigated by the brief ascendance of Evangelical piety; worse
still, such a step remained irrevocable when ex-slaves became 'uppity niggers'!

Feminist theologians have a great respect for Christianity's
healthy distance from trendy political whim. Women's history
teaches us that flirtation with expedient politicians can end in
betrayal. At the same time we draw much strength from the two-
centuries-long struggle for women's rights in the Western world.
We would never dismiss such events as transient, or make the more
far-reaching mistake of divorcing the sacred from the secular. We
would never deny God's 'right' to act in secular affairs. Opponents
of women's priesthood do the established church no good in claiming that a woman's vocation is brought about by an infatuation
with the hiccups of history.

One of the major contributions of the women's movement and
feminist theology is that its students are not ashamed to discuss
the human feelings that motivate much of what we do. The inter-
dependence of emotion and logic, scholarship and commitment,
need not take away from either the precision or the dedication that
is required of us at this time.

> Women's studies do not pretend to an ethical neutrality. This
> stance is actually a ruling-class ideology. Neutrality hides a
> commitment to the status quo. All liberation scholarship is ad-
> vocacy scholarship. This should not make it less objective . . .
> but this objectivity is in the service of passionate commitment.[7]

Feminist theology's eclectic methodology does not always corre-
spond to traditional academic divisions of knowledge. Poetry and
psychology can spill over into linguistics and political science. This
need not detract from either logic or precision, but arises from a
healthy distrust of being trapped into too narrow a definition of
ourselves or our individual tasks.

To see the fresh idealism of feminist theology as the ultimate corrective to the ills of the church or to see its insights as unprecedented would be an absurdly lofty claim. It is a fact, though, that people have come back or decided not to leave the church because feminist theology has made Christianity available to them again. It has given to some the strength to withstand the church's rejection of their gifts by providing new channels for them. This became abundantly clear as our letters flowed in:

> My awareness of the church and its meaning for me has been drastically changed by the women issue. My consciousness was changed as a consequence of a day school run by Una Kroll here at Leicester and subsequently reading Mary Daly's *Beyond God the Father*.

> When I first began to realise the extent and nature of this sexism about fifteen years ago I was very hurt and angry indeed and very confused: but slowly these *emotional* reactions have worn off. After all, despising the opposite sex is a game that two can play, though I don't recommend it . . . If one attends church is one supporting mainly Christ or phallic worshipping paganism? I haven't attended Mass for years though I am considering attending again. The problem is always whether to try to influence an organization from within, or leave it to avoid supporting a policy/concept or whatever with which one strongly disagrees.

> I am still a Christian largely owing to the valiant witness of Christian women around me since childhood.[8]

The components of feminist theology are not individually unique but the following combination is, we think, peculiar to contemporary feminist spiritual awareness and it is this combination that we are offering to theology today. What is emerging as positively characteristic of feminist theology?

First, it is both subjective and objective, both conceptual and personal. It is a study which confesses the importance of the lives of the students. The student's experience informs the structures that exist for study and plays some part in the process and problem of selection. Our studies are *communal* and above all co-operative, i.e., non-hierarchical. Theology is created when people congregate to listen to one another's dreams, hopes, fears and failings – and to hear God speaking in their midst.

We envisage this characteristic as a pinwheel spinning outwards from a strong centre, radiating ever outwards, circles within circles. Unlike the pyramidic structure of Hebrew, Pauline and Platonic thought, where God, Big Daddy, is on top, creator of man who rules over women, children and the rest of the creature kingdom, the circular model reflects the inner authority and language of mysticism itself as well as being the hall-mark of liberation theology. The language of the strong still centre is universally acknowledged and loved, whether it comes to us in the Fourth Gospel, Blake's grain of sand, the Mandala of Jungian thought or the small secret hazelnut beloved of Mother Julian – 'all that is made, made by love'.[9]

We cannot fail to be touched by these truths; neither can we avoid facing up to the realities of the pyramid as they bear down on us each day in school, medicine, in our work. As privileged people we take an 'acceptable level' of hierarchy as the way of the world, but the wretched of the earth know its violence and their own helplessness every day of their lives. The theology born of oppression questions whether this triangular assumption and model which undergirds Western culture in social, economic, political as well as religious spheres is a sound model for the survival of either the Christian community or the planet. So long as all our transcendental experience – prayer, contemplation, meditation – bears and reflects only an inner authority, so long as it is a personal preoccupation, then theology can never be a living entity in our lives or our thinking, and all our noblest efforts of social change and spiritual revival will be dedicated to the restructuring of the pyramidic lie. The alternative is not a rejection of transcendence or a new pantheism, or indeed the denial of the need for special roles. It is rather a recognition that the holding together of withinness and withoutness, immanence and transcendence, the particular and the universal, requires a cyclical and evolutionary rather than a vertical model.

Much as we revere the circle as a model of spiritual truth, we are wary when the balance tips towards anger, exclusivity and rejection. There are indeed those who adopt these stances, but it is vital to realize that they would also reject feminist theology itself as part of a tradition that needs to die. Mary Daly in her book *Gyn/Ecology* claims that part of a woman's effort at spinning her way towards freedom necessitates the shedding and total rejection of all the male-structured and male-controlled world. In support of her thesis she catalogues, with carefully researched accuracy, the historical horror stories – of genital mutilation, gynaecological experimentation, footbinding, suttee, Nazi torture of women – all practices invented by men to control and subdue women.[10]

Daly's stance is supported by Naomi Goldenberg, a psychologist and student of religion who sees the deep-rooted evil of sexism as irredeemable. In her book *The Changing of the Gods*, Goldenberg asserts: 'Scorn for the female in general and the female body in particular is a basic element in Christian practice and symbolism.'[11] She rejects any hope, put forward by feminist theologians, that Christianity can heal its dualistic split of body and spirit, and regards the work of theologians like Rosemary Radford Ruether as an attempt to appease tradition. Goldenberg sees the spectrum of religious feminist thought as ranging 'from those who revise to those who revolt – from those who would reform our present stock of images to those who have stopped searching the shelves of traditional religious warehouses of church, Bible or synagogue and are looking elsewhere'.[12] Any study undertaken in a commitment to Jewish or Christian faith is consigned to the revisionist end of the spectrum. Both Daly (more in anger than in sorrow) and Goldenberg (with a pitying and rather scornful backward glance) go on to create a new forum for a new women's religion.

Those revisionists who stay working as loyal dissenters within the church are sharply altering the questions that the church is having to ask about women. As late as 1948 a pamphlet was published entitled *The Role of Women in the Church*,[13] detailing all the subordinate roles women might fulfil in the church. Feminist theologians and others question the assumption that the roles must be subordinate. The question has changed in the last few years from: 'What work can women do, suiting their own special talents and training to a male orchestrated church?' to 'What can women do to cure the deep-rooted illness from which Christianity is suffering?' We can confidently claim that our interests and insights encompass a far wider range of possibilities than the question of ordination. It is important to reiterate, though, that traditional churchmen's suspicions of Christian feminism are nearly always expressed within this arena. Interest tends to begin and end with the threat of violating the inviolate sanctuary.

In this country, feminist theology has been instrumental in pinpointing the failure of the churches to recognize the urgency of the 'woman question' in church and society. Some feminist theologians feel the strong claims of vocation to the priesthood, most do not. The rejection of vocation by the institutional church has necessitated that we give a lot of thought and energy to a campaign that most of us regard with a good deal of impatience. We would really rather be celebrating women's contribution to theology than fighting for its liturgical recognition! However, the ordination issue is a symbol and a rallying point: tracts, pamphlets and sermons are passed from one woman, one group to another like telegraphed messages along the line of battle. More formal studies almost conceal their breadth of thought and the eminence of their writers by bold, lively and informal presentation.[14]

In the United States there is an abundance of more widely and lavishly published material and well supported research. Women's issues are well to the fore in mainstream theological exploration. Some of us beleaguered islanders are dedicated enough to send for the published material, but on the whole we read what we can buy here. We find that US feminist theology is both reflective of our ferment and instructive of it. The process of cross-fertilization is accelerating and is deeply encouraged by the ministrations of American women priests.[15]

We hasten to add, though, that here or 'over there', feminist theology is practical, not comfortably confined to pulpit or pedestal. It is predominately pastoral. At the heart of women's striving towards a workable theology is the realization that traditional religious thought often treats everyday experience as something apart from God's good creation. A point of view about the world comes from sharing both the ordinary and the extraordinary of our lives. We take up joyously the invitation given by John Robinson to create a truly lay and experiential theology:

> It is a call in the first place, not to relevance in any slick sense but to exposure, to compassion, to sensitivity, awareness and integrity. It is a call to bear reality, more reality than is easy or possible for a human being to bear unaided. It is to be with God in his world. And, in each epoch or culture, the place of the theologian is to stand as near as he may to the creative centre of God's world in his day.[16]

Robinson was to name this challenge 'open-cast' theology.

Another very important aspect of feminist theology is the way it emerges. It is episodic rather than systematic. Like the best of all myth and legend, it comes from people's stories. You will not need to read very far in the wide-ranging field of feminist writing to discover a great store of wisdom and, more revolutionary still, an exciting store of strength and vision from women, both articulate and tentative, who are learning to tell their stories to each other.[17] Narratives by women are notable for their virtual absence in scripture, so for women in the Judaeo-Christian tradition, where the process is explicitly informed and enlightened by prayer, this emergent quality is even more strengthening.

One of the women who wrote to us when we first imagined the need for this book said: 'He [our correspondent's spiritual director] would like me to write for publication but I cannot yet write in a detached academic way. I cannot abstract ideas from my own experience. Perhaps this is what the feminine has to contribute.'[18]

Church authorities have always drawn on the wisdom and insights of women. But those blessed and venerated by the church as wells of holiness have been set apart – in cloister like Teresa of Avila and 'little' Thérèse of Lisieux – or in self-imposed asceticism like Simone Weil and Mother Julian. These women have needed neither the priesthood nor the power of the institutional church. While we rejoice with all Christendom at their poetry and goodness, we are unhappy that their prophetic stature has so often been accorded them on the grounds of their self-effacement and humility rather than the truths they speak.

Such women were held up to both of us when first we began to gnaw at the question of priesthood for women. We were told that women like Evelyn Underhill, for example, had such a profound grasp of Christian truth that bishop and Pope alike were unfit to touch the hem of her garment. We began to wonder what sort of organization we were in when you had to be *that* good to be accorded the authority that we (rightly or wrongly) associated with priesthood, which you then really would not need. We say that the unworthiness of the minister does not hinder the grace of the sacrament, but with women it seems it must be either the pew or the pedestal.[19] The quiet serenity of the mystics can so easily become patronized, and pilgrimage can so often be to a truth we are too busy or too important to make our own.

In a sense it is true that the ultimate ambition of a Christian is to achieve sainthood, and for many this has involved seeking obscurity. What Christian can do other than respect the distinction between great goodness and (mere) greatness – the distinction between wisdom authority and status authority. 'The order of excellence and the order of achievement'[20] was how one of our correspondents put it. She is an art historian, and from the insights of her professional and Christian experience, she likens spiritual quest to the art lover's longing to paint just one definitive picture; a yearning of a totally different order than the mere ambition to become Director of the Tate Gallery. Veneration of the excellent, though, can turn into an Olympian disdain of the everyday need to exercise gifts of a humbler order. Most of us need a simple platform of some kind and could not exist in the rarefied air of the pedestal. It is hard for us not to be dismayed and diminished by women saints when they are held up not for our inspiration but to reproach us for our graceless, nagging demands. The Virgin herself is an eternal focus of this tension for women.

If accord for women is chained to traditional virtue – 'Be good, sweet maid, and let who will be clever' – it is clearly not so with men. For this reason we welcomed an editorial of *Theology* discussing the relationship of private behaviour and public pronouncement. John Drury examined Paul Tillich's demand that his career and status be protected from the consequences of his behaviour as an 'impenitent seducer'. Drury's balanced and merciful discussion – 'it must be better to value a man for what he can give rather than be obsessed by what he cannot'[21] – led us to ask ourselves what stature or mercy would have been accorded an *impenitent* Magdalene or Pelagia.

It is not therefore surprising that our own calendar includes a number of very secular saints. Christian feminism owes an incalculable debt to the many creative women who, tragically for the church, have had to use their energies outside. In spite of the institutionalized double standard, those who remain are no longer fearful of expressing a need for status or authority where it is felt, but the gulf between the institutional church and many great women living today seems vast.

One of the great triumphs of the women's movement, in and out of the church, is the deeply-felt insistence that there can be no gap between the tensions of private life and the ideology of religious or secular politics. The private is political. Jill Tweedie, reviewing a recently published book, wrote: 'Someone, somewhere, decides that a poorer quality lavatory paper is suitable for working men, where managing directors have their bottoms pampered. This small item says more about attitudes than any amount of careful words designed to ridicule the idea of workers' inferiority, and yet the workers, being men, were obviously ashamed of being reduced to this level of complaint.'[22]

She adds that any woman, especially within the women's movement, would uninhibitedly give this disparity its full significance. Our lives as women teach us that it is on this kind of level that the truth of fine speeches is tested. It is refreshing and hopeful to be able to admit the relevance of both emotion and soft toilet paper!

We see the need for the unique history of women's experience to be incorporated and recognized within the structure of the institutionalized church. We see the need for this emerging theology to be lifted liturgically by women priests.

Looking back on our adolescence, as we often did when shaping this book, the unquestioned feature of biblical study was that the stories were all by and about men. We found that at the time of learning we felt little anger at what we were taught. Of course God was a man. The Fall was woman's fault, brought about by Eve's lust of the eye, the lust of the mind for knowledge, causing her, not Adam, to bring misery to the garden. After all, women are by nature impetuous, sensuous, concupiscent. 'That's woman,' we thought, 'I don't like her much or trust her much, but since I am one I'd better make do with second rate.' We realize now that if the positive power of myth is about strengthening a people, then Judaeo-Christian women really got off to a bad start. Great explorations are taking place within Jewish feminism, too, and women are dusting off some remarkable treasures of hidden Jewish history[23] which we can use, expand and respect, confirming new-found vision.

Study in the language of sexism is another exciting area for Christian feminists. We are beginning to recognize the inescapable link between the use of words and the reality that use reflects in society. We are asking ourselves to what extent the language we use limits us in what we can dare to envisage. Some Christian feminists believe that it is vital to address God in a new way that does not limit the divine love and omnipotence to the human concept of fatherhood. No language can reflect God's greatness, but 'Father/Mother God' might begin to remove an obvious stumbling block without abandoning the language of nurture in our prayers as well as our theology.[24] This exploratory suggestion has provoked strong reactions from traditionalists in the august forum of the letters pages in national dailies. During the debate on women priests the same admonitory line was elevated to immutable truth. As if speaking on Jehovah's behalf, Graham Leonard, now Bishop of London, sagely warned against tampering with sexual symbolism. We are walking over the land mines of sexual symbolism to enter into the reality of sexist language. The explosions are unfortunate. We can only hope that our children will be able to tread the territory without the wounds and damage that we carry with us.

Eric Mascall, too, paraphrasing the Calvinist Von Allmen, stresses the latter's 'recognition that the polarity of human nature is not a superficial or accidental differentiation, primarily concerned with the propagation of the species, but penetrates human nature to its most *profound recesses*' (italics ours).[25]

Stern father says: 'Keep off, it's dangerous! You'll be sorry.' We say, 'Why not, Bishop? Why not, Father Mascall?' If status quo sexual symbolism perpetrates hatred of the body, subjugation of nature, fear of the unconscious, fear of any depth-dimension of women's spiritual experience – indeed, even if it only prevents us from receiving the longed-for ministrations of women priests, then we say it needs tampering with.

In doing theology and in finding our own names and stories, feminists who remain within traditional religious institutions have a Promethean struggle. Earlier in this chapter we outlined some of the directions women had taken in their despair at church or synagogue. There are in fact a wide range of alternatives to the church attempting to encompass the new consciousness of women in society. Apart from Judaeo-Christianity and the aforementioned range of matriarchal studies – witchcraft, goddess worship – the choices include depth psychology, Marxist feminism and consciousness-raising groups which depend on personal experience alone. This latter is a characteristically twentieth-century substitute for traditional religious expression, especially among middle-class people.[26]

We hope it is by now obvious that our own sympathies and fervent energies anchor us to the Christian faith. Participation in the rich possibilities of feminist theology makes us long for other women to remain within the structure of the church to breathe new life into it. Nevertheless, we disagree with the smug exclusivism of those who say that the women who have left are somehow not worth their salt.

The overwhelming task of feminist theology is, in our view, to face the fact that Christian theology is guilty of sexism, as it has been guilty of racism and classism, but also to affirm that this faith, this theology, is not irredeemably sexist. This is a critical mission within all organized religion.

Our theology is not concerned with the substitution of one tradition with another – replacing one half of human history with another. It is about claiming our tradition and reclaiming hidden history. It is about redeeming, resurrecting men and women to unforeseen possibilities. It is about restoring a balance, not a desperate search for a past or future Utopia. This means it can never be for women alone. Mary Daly once refused an interview with a male professor because she did not 'wish to dialogue with the oppressor'.[27] To exclude either the so-called enemy or the male-dominated woman from the opportunity to do theology would be anti-feminist. (Updated in preface to second edition, p. xviii.)

Like exponents of liberation theology and black theology, feminist theologians would like to be out of a job as soon as possible. Any notion of permanent cult and Vestal Virgins of a rarefied women's religion is taboo. Our hope is that mainstream theology will rise from these searing critiques to create a more just and life-loving world.

5

Daughters of the Promise

'If women have been faithful to any class of the human family, it has been to the Levite. The chief occupation of their lives, next to bearing children, has been to sustain the priesthood and the churches. With continual begging, fairs and donation parties, they have helped to plant religious temples on every hill-top and valley and in the streets of all our cities, so that the doleful church bell is forever ringing in our ears. The Levites have not been an unqualified blessing; ever fanning the flames of religious persecution, they have been the chief actors in subjugating mankind' (Elizabeth Cady Stanton, *The Women's Bible*).

'I would give her [the church] my head, my hand, my heart. She would not have them. She did not know what to do with them. She told me to go back and crochet in my mother's drawing room. "You may go to the Sunday school, if you like," she said. But she gave me no training even for that. She gave me neither work to do for her nor education to do it' (Florence Nightingale, *Letters*).

'If the ordination of women is the issue above all others that divides the church, then it deserves to be divided' (Polly Toynbee, *The Guardian*, 2 November 1977).

*   *   *

We want to be parochial in this chapter. We want to talk about clergymen, synods, the Mothers' Union, the cleaning of the brasses and the singing in the choir. Women are excluded from one vital area of the church's work – the ordained ministry – and many of those who urge their continued exclusion do so on the grounds that the church is unclear about the nature and purpose of priesthood, and that there must somehow be an attempt to 'sort it all out' before proceeding to widen it. Nobody ever seriously suggests that we should make any profound theological examination of the other activities mentioned above. Our Lord himself gave some pretty good guidelines in the parable of the talents and lamentably failed to give his followers practical advice about ecclesiastical closed shops that would inhibit our implementation of the lesson. Perhaps he never imagined it would be necessary.

As Christian feminists in a largely male-controlled church we share the dilemma about ministry, but see no hope for its resolution in present circumstances. We see feminist critique as vital in an examination of the meaning of priesthood, and shared priesthood as a primary pre-requisite for new life and mission in today's church. The models we use when speaking of our tensions and personal experience hold good in other Catholic and Reformed manifestations. The problem of sexism is with the entire Christian community. Studies of women ministers in other mainstream churches do not yet, in these early days, reveal any significant 'feminization' of the power structures.[1]

The resistance in our own (Anglican) church to shared priesthood and the meaning of that resistance is both symbolically and practically an important area to examine as we envisage a complete ministry. In the Church of England, the main body of resistance to women's ordination is amongst the clergy: they are the group who, constitutionally at least, are able to block progress in the ponderous workings of synod politics. In November 1978, the motion for women priests was passed overwhelmingly by the bishops and by a majority in the House of Laity. Clergy votes blocked and defeated the motion, and may well continue to do so in the future.[2]

Developments since November 1978 have been depressing. In July 1979, the Synod (same delegates) turned down a motion to allow women legally ordained overseas to function as priests in the UK, even with limited conditions and 'proper safeguards' (!). Choice memories of that debate, apart from a half-empty chamber until the vote, and rumours of champagne corks popping after it, include one cleric's likening the 1978 decision to a choice to be a 'non-smoking compartment'. The implications of that metaphor are staggering for women. We had become familiar with talk of pollution, and hints of menstrual uncleanness, but never before had we been part of a fight against cancer! Another startling statement came from one of our loving prudent fathers, who said that the ladies here in the UK with a vocation to the priesthood, whose hopes had been dashed, might be upset to find their overseas sisters supplanting them at the altar. To this remark, a woman veteran of Synod, Betty Ridley, remarked that the church needed the ministrations of women priests, not the protective gallantry of those who would prevent them.

Since an earlier Synod decision in 1975 stated that there were no fundamental theological objections to the ordination of women, one can deduce the state of limbo in which many women find themselves: 'It tells them that their sense of vocation might well be genuine, and won't be ungenuine because of their sex; and it tells them to wait . . . such a situation is a recipe for greater frustration and much individual suffering.'[3] In the winter of 1979, Robert Runcie was appointed as 102nd Archbishop of Canterbury; he has expressed opposition to women priests. In the autumn of the same year a new Pope who had seemed initially to show signs of breadth and flexibility in understanding other areas of human oppression said some definite 'nos' to the emancipation, both ecclesiastical and physical, of women (as well as subsequently threatening the teaching of two of the Catholic Church's finest theologians – Hans Küng and Edward Schillebeeckx). Can it be possible that Pope John XXIII could have said in 1963?:

> Since women are becoming ever more conscious of their human dignity, they will not tolerate being treated as more material instruments, but demand rights befitting a human person both in domestic and public life . . . Human beings have the right to choose freely the state of life which they prefer, and therefore the right to follow a vocation to the priesthood or religious life.[4]

What is this irresistible magnet of anti-feminism to which the church seems drawn in the 1970s and early 1980s – the decade of so much change and revelation for women themselves? That such radical and far-reaching thought and action will bring about a backlash is inevitable. But is it inevitable that the church should be a part of this? That it is, is clear in the simple fact that a special exemption clause had to be written, for the church, into the Sex Discrimination Act.[5] It is clear, too, in the thinking of many priests in the church. One of the most dramatic examples of this came from a priest who spoke against the motion in the 1978 Synod. Fr David Diamond of Deptford said that he was pledged to oppose the ordination of women out of loyalty to the dockers and working men in his parish. These men, said David Diamond, were feeling more and more insecure in a world of such rapid social change and economic stress, and needed the church's affirmation that the place for (their) women was in the home. The laughter that greeted this remark must have been painful for him, and we certainly felt it was more than a little unjust when there were so many equally chauvinistic but more cleverly disguised examples of prejudice that day. The warm and lively community that Fr Diamond has helped to build is witness to the fact that his wish to be 'alongside' the men in his parish is deeply felt and appreciated. Diamond's statement was important on two counts: he refrained from saying, as so many did, that the debate in that chamber had nothing to do with 'women's lib'. His honesty revealed some of the need, often unspoken, to appease and alleviate the alienation of working men that the Church of England has experienced since the Industrial Revolution. There is a great unresolved labyrinth of classism in our church, which *we* see as deeply connected to its sexism, and both are part of the centuries-long hardening of the division between laity and clergy.

These are among the many tensions that our clerical synod delegates take home with them as they leave the hothouse atmosphere of synod deliberations, to live out the undramatic realities of twentieth-century ecclesiastical life. The reality of priestcraft in Anglican parish life today means, in the main, that it is an uphill struggle to achieve a warm and lively church community if the vicar is no good! In parish life, the vicar is the person whose whole paid job is to reflect and express the corporate Christian experience in prayer, preaching and teaching. He is the main visitor of the sick. His task is to comfort the disturbed and, hopefully, to disturb the comfortable. The wider community meet him at dramatic and vulnerable times of their lives – at birth, marriage or bereavement. He may be a local amenity or a local landmark, and the mediaeval adage 'clerus Anglicanus stupor mundi' still often holds true among the faithful and the non-faithful alike. There are widely different ways of 'amazing the world' – by learning, diligence, eccentricity, ineptitude, incompetence – or just by that unique blend of other-worldliness and this-worldliness that people have remarked in the Anglican clergy down the ages. Even the most effective and dynamic lay initiative is enhanced by the vicar's affirmation, and to some extent impoverished without it. So far, so good – priestly leadership, with its accompanying training and vocation to serve the community in this way, is part of the sacramental ordering of the church – and the mental libretto of those who choose to ignore the song but need the individual singer from time to time. Special people to show that all people are special.

The negative side of this almost cosy picture is something which we must examine, and which we can only describe as institutionalized holiness. At various points in the history of the church and the consciousness of its individual members, the holiness (wholeness) and the spiritual reality that all Christians seek becomes, to a greater or lesser extent, the property of priesthood and the religious life. Clergy and cloister are regarded as powerhouses. The priest handles and distributes the 'holy things', the elements of sacramental life; the cloister is given over to prayer as its first priority. The representational nature of these functions is somehow lost in a miasma of imagined expertise. It does not really matter to what extent one holds the religious life in veneration, or whether one's view of priesthood veers towards the presbyterian or sacerdotalist ideal; monks, nuns, vicars, ministers and elders are all supposed to be 'souped-up' Christians.

The clergy are certainly seen by most radical feminists as being in the front line of the enemy ranks along with the even more powerful secular high-priests of psychiatry and medicine and their acolytes – health visitors and social workers: all those dedicated to a smooth running of society and sexual status quo. We who remain in the church must acknowledge the fact that there are and ever were priests of the church who have responded with unequivocal warmth and compassion to the pain and powerlessness of women, and felt their own priesthood to be diminished by the second-class citizenship of women in the church. But among the world's woes there are so many more dramatic calls for compassion and involvement. Good men and true tend to be bored and impatient with ecclesiastical politics, and many with vision are ground down with overwork. The twentieth-century way of stoning the prophets is to kill them with exhaustion.

As we labour away trying to work out legal and constitutional ways of achieving whole and shared priesthood, we know that it is the clergy we have to defeat. It is hard to speak lovingly and respectfully of them when they are such a powerful force to be reckoned with. We often create picture-poster images of goodies and baddies. Forgive us the indulgence of some rather schoolgirlish sketches, pinned up in our mental rogues' gallery. First on our 'Unwanted' list we present Father C. U. Tattanhall. He's an ecclesiastical John Wayne playing the Marshal. Part of cleaning up the town is keeping the womenfolk indoors, preferably having babies. He is prepared to lay his job on the line – take his Bible from the bed, his saddle from the wall and move on out along the line if the high-noon train brings the Kroll gang into town.[6]

Fr Tattanhall is likely to use the word 'priestess', invariably in

a derogatory way, to conjure up voluptuous images of naked
women and fertility rites. In fact, C.U. feels threatened by women
unless they are polishing the brass, but then again some would not
allow women into the sanctuary at all. Father T's very authori-
tarian figure can be found at the other end of the churchmanship
spectrum, too. There he wears a wider collar and shuns lace; and
the selective scriptural justifications for outlawing women priests
do not sound, from his fundamentalist tradition, quite so strange.
Fr Tattanhall may be married, happily or unhappily; he may be
gay. He may be both.

Another familiar figure on the scene of church politics is the
Reverend P. Lees-Later, who speaks of female ordination as some
sort of sad inevitability. His world is being ruffled by stroppy
women and, like King Canute's waves, they will have to be met
some time. 'Lord, make me clean, but not yet . . . please.' If Lees-
Later were on the synod, we can be sure that he would not have
voted in favour of women. He would probably have latched on to
the major neutral arguments – ecumenism or schism – with great
enthusiasm if with little conviction. P. Lees-Later prefers women
in their place, but it is possible for him to have good working
relations with successful career women such as teachers, nurses or
even social workers – those women he can define in a nurturing
and supportive role. There is great embarrassment in his life when
his good ladies step out of the stereotype.[7]

Then we have the Rev. I. M. Cumming. He always assumed that
women priests would arrive on the scene as of right and necessity.
His commitment to the 'greater' injustices of the world – apartheid,
hunger, political oppression – has made him unwilling to engage
in the passé struggle. Only the absurd shenannigans of 1978 have
dragged him to our aid. Church politics are boring and irrelevant,
but when they hurt and maim people, then I.M. will muscle in and
clean up the town a bit too. Give us a Rev. Cumming before he's
seventy and we've got him for life.

We had a good laugh creating these miniatures. More seriously,
we realize that this sort of humour is sometimes the only weapon
worth using. Other images come to mind – of workers blowing
raspberries at the gaffer behind his back, of children enjoying the
sound of naughty words in polite company, or of mediaeval arti-
sans turning the feudal lord's memorial bust into a gargoyle. Dood-
ling and caricaturing are a welcome relief from our more serious
task of trying to engage in fruitful dialogue with intransigent clerics

– plucking at their sleeves and feeling, as one correspondent put it, 'like sergeants in the officers' mess'.[8]

We make no judgments on these priests' prayer lives, their preaching, or the strength and nourishment of their pastoral ministries, and certainly not about the nature of their sexuality. Serious critique must, however, begin with the convoluted twisting of their theology on the issue of women priests. We assert that, in many cases, this has damaged their credibility both as seekers after truth and as upholders of distinctive tradition.

There is a healthy multiplicity in Anglican faith and practice, and a decision to join this particular church involved, for both of us, a certain amount of learning the landscape in order to appreciate its contours more fully. (The US half of this partnership came to Anglicanism not simply from the 'Bible belt', but from the fundamentalist Church of Christ – known as the *buckle* of the Bible belt. The UK half came, more typically but less dramatically, from a belligerently-held agnosticism, brought on by a surfeit of Sunday school and RI in the Anglican tradition, and enjoys, to this day, a long, though uneasy, honeymoon and rediscovery.) Emphasis on the Bible or tradition, word and sacrament (low or high), varies from community to community and from priest to priest. In finding space to practise it is important that individuals find a *place* to practise. This involves not a monochrome and rigid church-womanship, but a certain commitment in one's choice of tradition from which to explore and understand others. Work in the campaign for women's ordination has shown the whole thing to be turned, in certain instances, on its head – not in a sudden rush of brotherhood and togetherness, but in ways involving some alliances that look, from where we stand, far from holy. Clergymen, solidly and steadfastly implanted in Reformed certainties, can suddenly develop uncharacteristic attacks of 'ecumania' and demand that we do nothing without the solidarity of our brethren from Rome – let the scarlet woman without save us from the scarlet women within. On the other hand, a letter appeared in *The Times* in November 1978[9] from a high church priest, who, while rejoicing at the victory of his cause, chose to question the appointment and authority of the bishops who had voted in favour of women. The priest said the bishops had 'badly misjudged the mood of their lay people and clergy'.

Authority, obedience and emphasis on the apostolic claims of episcopacy were, we thought, strongly upheld by Catholic tradition. On no other issue do priests of this tradition question episcopal appointment and leadership; on no other issue do they take up a fundamentalist approach to the Bible; on no other issue has the crucial call to ecumenism been able to defeat the 'sacrificing truth for unity argument' so resoundingly that the second argument was hardly mentioned. To renege on one's theological tradition, not from a genuine change of mind but from professional and sectarian fear and self-interest, seems a dangerous kind of treachery.

We are told that the 'ambitions' of an estimated hundred or so women are nothing compared to the real possibility that, in our lifetime, we may achieve union with the Roman Catholic Church. The call for the unity of all Christendom is crucial, but we are often puzzled at the way the 'discipline of ecumenism' argument is used. The ordination of women, rather than papal authority, is often presented as the vital factor in Anglican/Catholic dialogue; yet Eric Mascall and other opponents warn about unseemly haste to 'get in before Rome does'. Indeed, the dramatically swelling call for women's ordination among Roman Catholics, lay and religious, is an embarrassment to their own establishment as well as ours. We are puzzled by the call to 'dialogue' and 'patience' from a man like the present Archbishop. The Most Reverend Robert Runcie has spent a good part of his life and scholarship in conversation with the Eastern churches, and yet his universalist stance has not yet brought him face to face with the fact that the Church of England is but one part of the Anglican Communion, *which already has women priests.*[10]

We find ourselves looking with an ironic eye at the wheeling out of Greek archbishops.[11] 'In the name of Mary,' said the late Archbishop Athenagoras, 'teach your women humility.' We view with some cynicism the *romanticizing* of the Greek Orthodox Church, held up to us by our own prelates as a repository of a magic and spirituality which we sorely need. How much of this is disingenuous – a kind of Thompson Aegean Tours view of spirituality? Whitewashed villages; black-clad, bearded, almost biblical figures – the myth of the Other and the Exotic-authentic. How much of all this is ill-disguised put-down? Is the humility of the Greek peasant woman really enshrined in the archbishop whose frequently extended ring she kisses and whose sanctuary she may not enter?

Opposition to women priests from members of the Catholic Renewal movement is almost universal. We find that our own emerging feminist theology draws us in the same direction. We, too, see the need for a re-assertion of the inestimable richness of sacramental life as a vital tool for the survival and mission of the church, and the inspired response to decadence, fear and alienation. The hostility and misogyny we encounter from members of this group is deeply wounding. The Catholic renewal movement so often seems to be concerned with externals such as clothes, priestly processions and authority structures, and is usually viewed with some amazement and lack of recognition by 'real' Roman Catholics. The Women's Movement is looking for symbol and beauty as spiritual wings to soar with: the church, at its best, is being enriched by the new insights and hope of liberation movements — of race, class and sex. A long-time champion of both secular liberation and women's ordination wrote: 'It is because the church should operate and, in some respects, still does operate at a deep psychic level that it is so vital for it to move into the future and to bring to it, not the stones of ecclesiastical tradition, but the bread of a living faith.'[12]

We have listened to many clergymen describing their training, and many are deeply disturbed at the kind of arrogance they are encouraged to feel. The institutionalizing of holiness, the sexism and classism that disable the church today, have all become enshrined in the training and expectations of young ordinands. We examined some of the material, past and present, that is used in the training of priests. We found ourselves thumbing through Fr Belton's *Manual for Confessors*.[13] We use it here because we are assured that it has commanded wide respect and influence. Father Belton's general description of the purpose and meaning of the sacrament of confession is beyond reproach. However, when describing the application of this knowledge to female parishioners, Fr Belton says:

> In hearing the confessions of the opposite sex, the priest ought to observe caution. His manner should tend to dignity and even to sternness, rather than to familiarity and pleasantness. He should avoid all unnecessary talk, and should suppress the tendency some women have of prolonging the confession by seeking advice on all kinds of subjects. There is a type of pious female who delights in long 'spiritual talks' when she comes to confession, and the more the inclination is indulged the worse she becomes. We have already mentioned that the priest should always avoid looking directly at the penitent, either when she is making her confession or when he is giving his advice. If

questions have to be asked on sins contrary to holy purity, the
confessor must take care not to put any questions which might
be so misunderstood as to injure his good name or bring the
sacrament into disrepute. When he has to hear a woman's
confession after dark, if it is at all possible he should arrange a
third party to be present . . . he should avoid all familiarity,
particularly with young women: he should not accept the presents they are all too ready to shower upon him.[14]

Clearly the liberating power of confession is severely impeded by
the gender of the penitent.

It has been well said that the religion of one age is the entertainment of the next. It would be unfair to hold up something so
prudent and antiquated for mere ridicule if we could be sure that
such a view of women, prurient, clinging and infantile, no longer
prevailed. The overwhelming impression, though, on reading this
sort of material is one of sadness. Fr Belton's strictures show a
fear-full misogyny that would probably not deny, if pressed, the
insistence on spiritual sexual equality demanded by the Christian
gospel, but the kind of gentle contempt that is truly and inevitably
brought about by over-familiarity. The women, the pious, the old,
the querulous we indeed have *always* with us. Fr Belton was being
practical: in the set-up he was writing for, the penitents would
have been at least 80% female, and the experience and sense of
failure brought about by a being cut off from the more robust lives
(and sins) of working men is evident throughout the book. We
heard in the Synod pleas of Fr Diamond an anxiety to address the
insecurities of his Deptford (male) parishioners – in his case, in a
successful bid for a truly mixed community. How else is Fr Belton
to account for the fact that the church seems entirely peopled by
pious old ladies but by blaming those ladies themselves? 'One feels
certain that one reason why priests fail to get men to go to frequent
confession is because they take so much time giving advice to pious
females that the men make the long wait an excuse for staying
away from the sacrament.'[15] The truth is, of course, that working
men stay away, not only from the sacrament, but from all church
worship. A common way of dealing with this unpalatable fact is
to retreat into prejudice and entrenched positions of superiority:

'How is the church to get the men?' is a very common question
. . . Almost always the various reasons try to find something
wrong with the church to account for the matter. I, personally,
have always felt that there is quite another side to the question

and that something is really radically wrong with the men. The greatest mistake the church has made in the matter seems to me that she has treated the men as if they were quite different from the rest of mortals, and has pandered to them in the most hopeless way . . . And all the time the British working man has been laughing up his sleeve. He knows perfectly well (for he is an honest, frank and charming fraud) that the real reason why he does not go to Church is because he is too lazy either to think or to get up in time.[16]

People of the 1980s cannot allow themselves Fr Belton's comfortable assurances. Brave and thoughtful endeavours; successful and unsuccessful appeals to deaf ears have been made before and since the time that his book was written. Church history as a whole includes many clerics and theologians who have honourably resisted such defensive resort to stereotypes. What other church can boast of the kind of golden age that seventeenth-century Caroline theology conferred on a largely deaf and ungrateful culture? Who could have expected the succeeding century with its sad decline in sensitivity and spirituality to have yet produced a William Law or a John Wesley? Or who, indeed, on first encountering the Anglican clergy in some of those stern faces on the Poor Law boards could foresee the Second Spring, the sanctity of the Clapham Sect, and the unnumbered heroes of many Victorian slum parishes? It is not enough to cry either 'sexist' or 'Tory party at prayer' without both paying tribute to the richness of priesthood where it is to be found in its great diversity, and by understanding where power has been compounded by deprivation and passivity to make the salt lose its savour. In our own time, movements such as Industrial Mission, Liturgical Renewal and the many widely-publicized and shared theological ferments of the 1960s have made some inroads into the problem of classism in the church. But the lay/clergy division is still very much with us, and the elevated status of the parson can inhibit his ministry in many vital areas. Institutionalized holiness has deeply eroded the soul of the church in ways that are not easily altered by either sociological change or smart sociological understanding. We found this account from one of our correspondents very helpful:

'For historical reasons, they [she is speaking of Roman Catholic and Anglican priests] are imprisoned in another way – they have been cast as teachers, leaders, guides and confessors to the Christian flock and isolated in that position. The laity expects them to be different, but worse, to be infallible. To meet these expectations, certain psychological adjustments have to be made – not always helpful to the person making them. If one knows one is not infallible, as all sane people do, yet is faced by a group of people expecting one to take responsibility and to act on their behalf, then one finds oneself needing props which can lead to self-deception. The situation is self-perpetuating. The easiest way out is to find someone _less_ good, _less_ able, on whom to project one's feeling of inferiority and failure. Woman has fulfilled this role from Eve onwards.[17]

This sympathetic description is one of many ways of looking at the stultifying effects of paternalistic priesthood, and a description that makes a lot of sense in the Anglican Church today, whose congregations remain heavily weighted towards female membership. 'The women we have _always_ with us,' the men having voted with their feet against further hierarchies ruling their lives, outside the necessary weight of those they must endure in factory, works and office.

An important theological reflection of this quandary is the struggle for new language to describe Lordship and the claims of the ultimate authority of love. A church that so many outside see as living off the fat of its past glories can seem to have no words left and no authority that has not become tainted with worldly power.

It was not always so, we imagine, in the early struggles. The Judaeo-Christian experience of God, born and nourished in a pre-literate nomadic setting and recorded for us in scripture, relates that there were times when the chosen bearers of the divine purpose were very few, pitted against a hostile counter-culture. There were times, too, even then, when the people of God made and controlled the culture we lived in. Who knows which of the two we are living in now? Are we 'taking ease in Zion' or 'singing the Lord's song in a strange land'? Probably both. The stumbling block is always the nature of power. 'But you are not to be called rabbi, for you have one teacher and you are all brethren. And call no man your father on earth, for you have one Father, who is in heaven. Neither be called masters, for you have one master, the Christ. He who is greatest among you shall be your servant' (Matt. 23.8–12). If this central teaching of Jesus had been maintained, the very foundations of hierarchy and authoritarianism in biblical religion would have been uprooted. The prophets of each generation have sought to restore the vision of Christ. Many of these have been in the ranks of the priesthood, and have cared for their people with a dove-like gentleness, emptied of power and paternalism. The church which Christ established, which spread dramatically in spite of persecution, soon found itself coming to terms with respectability and establishment. The blessing of the great Constantine in the fourth century is seen by many as the point at which it 'all began to go wrong' – when Mammon found a place in heaven and we set off along the primrose path, racketing along to the tune of 'The Vicar of Bray'. 'Whom the gods would destroy, they first make sentimental.'[18] Many a wise man has pointed out the dangers of nostalgia for the first century – of sighing from the polished pew for the lakeside of Galilee. When all the words in the world have been said on the subject, we are left with the knowledge that sin and culture have to be given equal weight. Or, as the compilers of the *Book of Common Prayer* more lyrically stated, 'there was never anything by the wit of man so well devised, or so sure established, which in the continuance of time hath not been corrupted'.

The work of exploring the poetry and profundities of the faith, begun by St Paul and the early Fathers, was the backcloth of mediaeval culture – when to faith was added, layer by layer, structure and dogma. Religion *was* the politics of the period. No church, no literacy; no chance either for women to opt out of biology except through the taking of vows. Some of the colourful figures that come tumbling into our minds – Chaucerian poor, pious priests and wicked worldly monks – belong to an all-powerful church which for hundreds of years was mother, teacher and welfare-worker for its people. 'I will return to my old convent,' says Heloise, 'and he (Abelard) shall become a priest. Outside the church, there is no advancement for any man, however great a genius he may be.'[19]

In more recent, post-Reformation history, the clerically dominated church has retrenched and shifted its power in people's lives. Learning and patriarchy have been joined by social privilege to implant the clergyman firmly in the professional middle class. Holiness has not only been institutionalized; it has been built into a career structure. When Heloise spoke her own doom, she saw the church as the only real cradle for Abelard's genius. Young men today talk about 'going into the church' as if it were an institution like the Stock Exchange.

John Robinson questions present-day patterns:

Reacting from the abuses of the Middle Ages, when multitudes of very mundane clerks were in Holy Orders, the Reformers entrenched the professional lines even further. In fact, it is very difficult to read the Ordinal of the Church of England without seeing it as a commissioning of a full-time professional clerisy. Indeed the connection between ordination and a living, as its natural goal and climax, has bitten deep into the whole psychology of the Church of England, and with it the baleful effects of another line which I have called 'the great benefice barrier'.[20]

We would hope that the ordination of women would contribute to widening patterns of ministry, and while we see no reason why there should not be a woman on the episcopal bench, this is in no sense a political aim. Women seeking ordination are not asking for ivy-clad rectories or assured careers, and would agree with Robinson as he continued:

> Rather I should wish to question more fundamentally whether ordination in any of our churches should ever include a built-in guarantee of £1,000 per annum for life. The church should remain entirely free in this matter and make it clear from the beginning that ordination is a calling and not necessarily a profession.[21]

Since the Industrial Revolution, the church has experienced a loss of political power; this process has been accelerated by the state's take-over of educational and welfare institutions. The church has found itself increasingly relegated to the private sector of life and morality, and its public role limited to that of adding colour and solemnity to great national occasions (as well as adding a few of its own). The parson or prophet today so often finds himself called to speak of the love and comfort in the gospel and to leave its wider social and political challenges to the experts. He will find admonitions not 'to step out of line', either in the high-minded strictures of somebody like E. R. Norman,[22] or in the mere day-to-day expectations of many colleagues and parishioners, who 'can't stand parsons meddling in politics'. Savonarola has become not Malcolm Muggeridge as much as Mary Whitehouse. Twentieth-century man's view of God the stick, God the carrot and God the friendly bobby on the corner, is hurtful to those who work for him full-time.

The private morality and domestic virtue that clergymen are expected to uphold are seen by society at large to be the proper sphere of women, and a hidden component of ecclesiastical opposition to shared priesthood is a real fear of the church's weakness – a fear that it has become too feminized already.

> The state projects all the virtues of compassion, caring for the young, gentleness, charity, generosity, vulnerability or 'openness' on to women, or into the private world of 'the Home', thereby privatizing morality so that it can make its political decisions without moral encumbrances. In the same way it projects these attributes on to the church – so that, ironically, the church to all political intents and purposes occupies the same place as women in society, insofar as it does not have to be seriously reckoned with in moral terms, but exists merely to sanctify the existing order or deal in a realm which is broadly termed 'spiritual'.[23]

The above description can be sharply experienced in parish life today in the attitudes of 'rational' men and women who visit the church at emotionally charged moments of private or corporate life. There are times when joy and anguish break the bounds of individual self-sufficiency – the birth of Jesus or a modern human baby, the loss of a cherished life (Lord Mountbatten's, or that of a close relative). At moments like this there is a turning, however nominal, to the church; when the sovereignty of Christ is given some honour and space. Feelings of great solemnity can bring forth a touching openness to the Christian gospel and present real opportunities for mission. Sadly, these precious times are often marred by a gentle bullying of the Christian family to stay where they are, somehow to become a tableau – like a school nativity play – to which a sentimental pilgrimage can be made by our enlightened elders and betters without a jarring of the nerves to inhibit the voluntary suspension of disbelief.

This is no place to explore the contemporary language/liturgy debate, but we do need to look seriously at the claims of those outside the church who believe, encouraged by their supporters within the church, that their eminence entitles them to dictate Christian forms or worship which they do not choose to share. If Christ's church and his gospel have no other claims to make apart from being an ecclesiastical theatre, like a holy version of the Royal Shakespeare Company at Stratford, where the best of English liturgical language can be heard and experienced in the proper setting, then it should not matter to those outside whether its deluded adherents worship in grunts and sign language! It is actually true that the Christian community could leave the theatre and the scripts to the truly 'cultured' and still, to their own amazement, survive.

The Church of England as a great national institution, inextricably bound up with history and pageantry, is a mixed blessing. It has been burdened with the weight of Establishment that has hung like an albatross around its neck. With such an anomalous method of appointments we should be grateful for the richness and diversity of priesthood and leadership that we do have. With such a minefield of vested interests to be negotiated, we could easily have produced a grey, cardboard collection of clerics. It may have at times seemed, as it was said in the last century, that 'the Church of England no power on earth can save',[24] yet it still miraculously survives, as bruised by its defects as it has been blessed by its prophets.

And what of the women? Who are they? Are they really pious and invisible nurturers of a priesthood and leadership they cannot share – 'the ladies, God bless them!'? Or are they the dispossessed daughters of Eve, whose carnality induces panic – 'the women, God help us!'? Ladies first – or rather, the women that we have always with us. Not all Christian leaders have either felt or shown Fr Belton's weariness with the virtuous sensibilities of his predominantly female clientèle. But even those who experience real vocation to this area of human need, refreshment and joy in fulfilling it would ask themselves some searching questions about the nature of clerically-dependent female piety.

Is the receptivity shown so much more widely by women to paternalistic patterns of priestly ministry an infantile dependence on Daddy – a Daddy who must be pleased and appeased? This would certainly be a widely-held twentieth-century explanation. Answers from various schools of psychiatry would be readily forthcoming to help individual women shed their deep-seated and childish unresolved patterns. Or is it true, as many suspect, that women actually are more pious and more open to the gospel message, more ready to receive the kingdom as a little child? Or are they, as many feminists claim, the cosmic underdog – the 'nigger of the world' – because female oppression undergirds all known human culture? If the latter is true, then women are truly the church – 'the subjugated people who have been lifted up by the emptying out of God's power in Jesus . . . the poor, the nobodies of earth.'[25] Jill Tweedie in *The Guardian* gave a succinct outsider's view: 'Women are the real Christians, men choreograph the special effects.'[26]

In any of the above conjectures (and all are to some extent true), the overt second-class citizenship of women in the churches is based on an anthropology of female inferiority – real or imagined – personally experienced or imposed from outside the self. Or, in the third case, on a romantic mythologizing of the underdog: an implication that continued openness to Christian truth depends on continued subjugation. There is no evidence in the gospels that the wretched of the earth will have to stay wretched in the kingdom of heaven, or that weakness and passivity are permanent partners.

More crudely, it is often implied that men, being naturally less devout, find it harder to remain active in the churches if their *exclusive* props, status and functions are denied them. It is often said in discussions about women priests, servers, choristers or sidesmen that if 'you let the women in, the men will all drift away' (from these jobs). This has, in our experience, sometimes proved to be true. We would not dismiss men as mere choreographers. But we would claim that the exclusiveness of the priestly function casts its shadow over the delights and duties of other church work. The sexual symbolism of the sanctuary filters down not so much 'through the ranks' as from the sanctuary down through the nave. It is fairly common for women to serve as sidesmen, and a congregation that held on to this anonymously dressed and very practical role as a male prerogative would be considered old-fashioned or eccentrically 'high'. Female servers, on the other hand, dressed in quasi-sacerdotal surplices and stationed 'up there' in the sanctuary, are the hall-mark of progressive liturgical attitudes in an Anglican community.[27]

We have both experienced a congregation with an all-male – in one case paid – church choir. The rationale and symbolism here is more complex. The figure of the choirboy with his angelic, scrubbed, yet glowingly mischievous face is universally beloved, if the design and sale of Christmas cards are anything to go by, in a way that no choir girl could hope to equal. There are those who claim, against all technical musical evidence, that this mystique is a matter not of youth, sweetness and clarity but of gender: that the 'ethereal' innocence and 'purity' of the childhood voice is only perfected in that of the young boy. As mothers of sons and daughters, with a boy chorister apiece, and as lovers of church music, we are glad that this artistic sexual apartheid is breaking down across the country. How long will this take, though, in the institutions which claim to uphold the highest standards and have schools set aside to train boys?

In the many debates we have witnessed on this issue of women priests, we have found that the last argument to present itself – either from the opposition or from our supporters who counsel patience – is that 'the women themselves don't want it'. Opposition to changing the sexual status quo from women members of the church is an important, though rapidly diminishing, area to be considered. An organization like the Mothers' Union, an area within Anglicanism where women's voices are heard and seriously attended, is generally viewed as a repository of traditional femininity and contentment. However much the Mothers' Union may be the butt of fashionable radicals, it is a world-wide, successful movement containing some remarkable women, and wields considerable power in its chosen and ceded spheres of influence. The MU is regarded by the hierarchy with an approbation ranging from uneasy tolerance to warm encouragement, and by its many members as their natural spiritual home, speaking to their all-absorbing tasks in a way that mainstream church-going does not.

A critique and understanding of the purposes of the Mothers' Union can be helpful in defining the fear and suspicion that exists between traditional churchwomen and the monstrous regiment of Christian feminists who either stay outside the church or only manage to hang on by the skin of their teeth. The Women's Movement posits a way of life that does not yet exist. The lack of meekness and the vigorousness of the language of contemporary feminism can be deeply threatening to those whose church affirms wifely, mothering and enabling roles in a way that secular society does not. Though Christianity has for centuries denigrated marriage as second-best and specified celibacy as holier and higher for its clergy, it has always been strong on monogamy and thus afforded this real protection to women and their children. For many this is grace sufficient at a time in our history when traditional values and family life are threatened as never before. 'If you want to be a liberated woman in the church, join the Mothers' Union,' says Rachel Nugee, MU Central President and a good friend of ours. Indeed, some of the work of the MU – such as caravan schemes, holidays for pressured mums, the 'message home' project for troubled young people in major cities, worship services geared to babies and toddlers – reflects the strong self-help orientation of many secular feminist projects. The difference in the two kinds of work conducted by these groups lies in their divergent visions of female destiny and responsibility, both of which lie in the movement's philosophical and historical roots. The history of the Mothers' Union is deeply rooted in loyal church membership. A historical survey and commentary on the Mothers' Union acknowledges the benevolent ghost of Mary Sumner, the founder of the movement, with her own perfectly happy marriage, pervading the spirit and vision of the MU today. 'We think this is worth referring to because it may be that her own happy experiences and the marriages of her parents and herself (Mary Sumner's father and husband were clergymen) made it difficult for her to have a sympathetic understanding of the position of those whose marriages were less successful, and that other members of the MU similarly blessed have sometimes had similar difficulty.'[28]

The wider women's movement today draws much of its inspiration from the feminist movements of the eighteenth and nineteenth centuries, in which a critique of patriarchal religion and the patriarchal family played a vital part. As we have seen, many of the early women's movement leaders were religious; loyal wives and mothers, their thoughts and writings contained a lively (and healthy) strain of anti-clericalism. Women in the feminist movement today, while sharing the concern of their Christian sisters for the chaos wrought by widespread marital breakdown, would nevertheless see the major problem to be the in-built injustices of the institution of marriage itself, injustices perpetrated by ecclesiastical dogma. All but a virulent minority of feminists would acknowledge the personal pain involved in families breaking up, but would claim that things will probably have to get worse before they get better. Nora really does have to slam the door of *The Doll's House*[29] and fight for her own identity before there can be any true peace – at home or in church.

Mothers' Union members of the church are deeply disturbed at this radical feminist line and do not seriously question the political context of marriage. In fact, the MU defines its function as upholding and supporting marriage, and has purposely self-limited its aims to a commitment to family stability as part of a 'children first' mandate. A major (and acknowledged) weakness of the Mothers' Union, and one that destroys its credibility with the many women outside its ranks, is its clerical dependence. The good-will of the vicar, and the support of his wife if he has one, is considered crucial in the setting up and work of an MU branch. Recent changes in MU constitution and practice attempt to spread the leadership and responsibility more widely, but there is a lack of the necessary political awareness needed to fight élitism, and so grass-roots leadership is slow to become a reality. The MU is deferred to by the ecclesiastical establishment in such matters as religious education, issues of remarriage and divorce, and problems of child-rearing and adolescence, where it conducts thoughtful and well-researched debate. The MU can justly be said to assume monopoly attitudes, a disadvantage that it shares with Anglicanism generally!

Mrs Sumner's tranquil dreams of a deepening spiritual dynamic to the joys and stresses of family life have become a lively reality, and have given confidence to many women, all over the world. But even in her own time, MU ideology must have seemed strangely remote to many of Mrs Sumner's contemporaries; to those women who were fighting for a minimum decency in their lives in the midst of the appalling injustices and exploitation of child and female labour. Feminists point out that the myth of fragility, femininity and the sacredness of family life were thought far too fancy to be wasted on the poor by the Victorian (often upright and Anglican) entrepreneur needing a pool of cheap labour. In the same way, the MU is seen by many women today to be addressing one part of the female experience and creating a norm of happiness and creativity that is simply not matched by the reality of many women's lives. When accused of domesticated Utopianism, the MU replies that the church needs to hold up ideals of motherhood and marriage at this time. Feminists and others, while not quarrelling with the need for vision, would find that the way forward lies not in simply 'upholding' institutions like marriage but in redeeming them from patterns of subservience and domination, and that goes for other aspects of the Christian life too. As this begins to come true we imagine and pray that the 'separated sisters' will have a good deal to say to one another!

The traditional female role that the church upholds in its teachings is widened in parish life to include the more public work of the church community. While we personally have a secret penchant for some of these time-honoured feminine activities like flower arranging and brass cleaning, there is considerable evidence from our letters that many women in the church are not happy with the spheres of work they are customarily offered. This letter was typical of many instances of incipient pew revolt:

> The talents you have to offer may be the more traditional ones of visiting and befriending, presiding over the tea-pot and the cake stall, taking round the magazine and endlessly raising money. I am not decrying these since they are still needed in

abundance. However, your particular talent may be reading and speaking in public, leading folk in prayer, looking after money, acting in an official capacity, chairing committees rather than writing the minutes – generally thought more appropriate for males according to C of E practice. How much encouragement, opportunity or training would the average lay woman get to use these abilities?[30]

The church does indeed need money, and this vital work is heavily under-pinned by female labour, as Elizabeth Cady Stanton pointed out. Many church people, priest and lay person alike, find the business of plant and upkeep tedious, but fund-raising certainly takes on some moral weight when it comes to giving money *away*. Bring and buy sales, or jumble sales, are a chore, but hard-hearted resistance is almost impossible when they are a way of contributing to Christian Aid and welfare programmes.

The life of the church is not, of course, entirely taken up with Autumn Fayres, stewardship campaigns and women's groups. The prime mission of the Christian community is to celebrate life in its liturgy. It is only fair to balance the picture of the value and enviability of traditional female activity with the fact that the humble enabling tasks and the trivial round are not what we celebrate at our most triumphalist. The big-bang church services are, in the main, in celebration of priesthood, buildings and leadership. It is at ordinations, inductions and consecrations that we find robes, processions and trumpet fanfares. Here in North-West London recently, we had a lavish dedication service of a new re-organized episcopal area! Church leaders protest that the church is not about organization and bishops, but liturgical emphasis would strongly indicate otherwise. We do not go in much for prestigious occasions and avoid them where possible. We would be more likely to feel like raising the roof at the baptism of a child than the baptism of a roof, but there is some substantial indication from our letters that many women in the church do find a lack of affirmation and participation in liturgy painful. We are brought back full circle to the symbolism of the sanctuary and pew. Christian feminist critique regards the alienation of the New Woman in old forms of worship as an important area for restoration.

As I sit in the pew, week after week, facing a sanctuary populated exclusively by males, listening to lessons read, sermons preached, prayers led by one male after another, except for the token woman from time to time, I begin to understand why the girl confirmees, more numerous than the boys to start with, gradually lapse. The boys act as crucifers, the girls help in Sunday school or Sunday group (i.e. mostly not in church) ... At our church if you are a girl and you cannot or do not want to ... look after young children, you rapidly become a listener, then, a non-listener and then a non-attender.[31]

How is the Anglican church to 'amaze the world' and the woman of the year 2000? Or even the departing daughters of the above parish? We ourselves resist an occasional urge to join their ranks, for reasons we expand on in the next two chapters. Nevertheless, sitting through the Synod deliberations of 1978 and 1979, and our subsequent forcible ejection from St Paul's Cathedral,[32] were distressing experiences. We confess to having had an initial impulse, in 1978, to dispose personally of the whole problem by inserting this announcement in *The Times* obituary column:

On November 8, quietly and peacefully, of heart failure, the Church of England, after protracted illness. Mourned and deeply loved by many.

Instead we have chosen to fight on. In saying 'no' to women's ordination, the church symbolically says 'no' to a vision that has taken root in the hearts and lives of a great many Christian women. That 'no' continues to reinforce the disturbing patterns that we have outlined in this chapter. Our fight for women's priesthood, which we have chosen as a liturgical reality in our own lives anyway,[33] is but one part of a larger crusade to restore the men and women of the church to the liberation promise of the Christian gospel. A few token women absorbed into largely unquestioned structures is no more a guarantee of the true feminization of the existing order than a woman Prime Minister. 'Clericalism is sexism raised to the second power'[34]: the models of ministry, language and organization used by the church today for its worship and mission are patriarchal. Our prayer is that they are not irredeemably patriarchal; in the present and future world this may as well read 'irredeemably defective'.

6

Daughters of the Reformation

'Mr Collins, you must marry. A clergyman like you must marry. Choose properly, choose a gentlewoman, for my sake and for your own. Let her be an active useful sort of person, not brought up high but able to make a small income go a long way' (Jane Austen, *Pride and Prejudice*).

'The previous Reformation did nothing to convince women that they were not second-class citizens in the Kingdom of God – except to allow them to become clergy wives. Then, no doubt it did not matter greatly whether they were convinced or not. But now it is vital' (John A. T. Robinson, *The New Reformation?*).

'This quiet dust
Was gentlemen and ladies . . .' (Emily Dickinson).

*   *   *

When a book, a play or an event in real life is likened to a vicarage tea party, the experience is immediately labelled as something wholesome, respectable and comically dull. A play that makes *Lady Chatterley's Lover* seem like tea on the parsonage lawn holds promises of raw and earthy reality. How hard it is to remember that the presence of the parson's wife – sitting so serenely pouring out the tea – was a matter not only of scandal but a direct result of turmoil and revolution! Who would have thought, when the dust had at last settled over the Reformation and the Puritan revolution following it, that that most notorious of females – the 'prieste's woman' – would come to represent all that is most decorous and proper in our national life: so much so that she has come to find a place of her own on the comic stage? Felt-hatted, thrifty and practical, an altogether more stolid and functional presence than her other-worldly, benign and dotty stage husband, the parson's wife often doubles as the Local Dragon or Lady of the Manor.

Media experts claim that there is no such thing as a media myth, that a stereotype has no hope of persisting for more than two years without some very real grounding in reality. It is not our business here to prove or disprove this, but it does seem fair to assume in a clerically-dominated church that the marriages of the priests in that church will reflect in some measure the strengths and weaknesses of its vision of marriage as well as the character of its ministry. When we started this project, we found that a substantial proportion of our letters came from the wives of priests. Many lively women are voting with their feet against the prevailing and unchanging patterns of patriarchal ministry, and it is therefore not surprising that those who cannot easily leave will be those who spearhead the fight for equal partnership.[1]

As happy camp followers ourselves, we would be dishonest not to declare our autobiographical interest in this subject. Our own emerging feminist theology teaches us that the lives of the students inform and structure the areas they choose to study. This chapter chose us long ago. It would be pointless to suggest that our lives and thoughts are not governed by the day-to-day realities of living over the shop, and ungrateful not to own the invaluable help of theologically-trained, ordained partners. We would hope that the Christian feminist critique of clericalism is deepened rather than blunted by truly loving the enemy! Although we do not share the gloomy prognosis of many of our sisters in the women's movement who declare the church to be beyond hope, we take a lively interest in the corollary to their assumption: if the parson is an anachronism and an irrelevance, where does that leave his wife? The one remaining member of the congregation? Should she continue to nurture the institution that is inseparable from the person she loves? What part can she play in the rescue and restoration of the institution? Or indeed, has the part she may well have played heretofore contributed to the enhancement or to the defectiveness of the priestly ministry?

Interesting as all these questions may be to us personally, they do not constitute reason enough for us to study them in these pages. What we as daughters of the Reformation do want to explore is the Reformation itself: its causes and aftermath, its triumphs and limitations. We believe such an exploration will throw some light on what is one of the most painful aspects of the church for many women: *wives, as such, have become too im-*

portant. Let us explain. One of the most vaunted enlightenments of the Reformation is that it restored marriage to a long-lost degree of spiritual dignity. The end of compulsory clerical celibacy was undeniably an important sign of a changed theology of sexuality. But when the church made a place for the loyal wife by the side of its priesthood, the seeds were sown for the vulnerability of both the clergy wife and the women who do not marry. The 'domesticity rules' ethos of parish life, and the single woman, traditionally excluded from it, can present a depressing picture. It is as if Eve were allowed back into the garden just so long as she took the rest of those offending apples and made them into chutney for the bazaar!

Several years ago, Janet Spedding, a doctoral candidate at Sheffield University, made a study of clergy wives in the West Riding of Yorkshire.[2] Many interesting and some quite unexpected attitudes emerge from this study. Reality and stereotype matched with surprising accuracy in the clergy wives she interviewed. She was accused by several feminist colleagues of studying a group and a subject which are both trivial and idiosyncratic, and found it necessary to justify her choice of subject matter. Justification, it seems, is the key word with regard to this subject. If the clergy marriage is a model which still contains many of the more traditional female expectations of the man/woman partnership, then feminists and others should be grateful to us for existing as a threatened species, all ready and available as research material! There are a good many theological and historical reasons for the cultural distancing of this particular group of women from the many waves of female awareness that have swept over our lives since the Reformation. Here it seems that those outside and inside the church regard clergy wives as a special case; in addition, in most instances the wives justify the category assigned to them. The search for a balance between service and self-realization is fraught with difficulties.

No other group of women expects their lives to be so totally circumscribed by the work of their marriage partners. Some clergy wives claim to this day that their 'profession' is a twenty-four-hour-a-day job. 'We're parson's wives twenty-four hours out of twenty-four. We breathe, eat and sleep the demands of our profession. We cannot shed our responsibilities when the clock says 5.30, or lay down tools at the sound of a hooter. Yet, merely because our husbands wear their collar the other way round, we, simple souls that we are, swear our lives away the moment we say "I will".[3] In spite of the fact that this letter was written in the 1950s, the tone of weary but good-humoured resignation is typical of many vignettes by and about clergy wives to be found today in women's magazines and the popular press. An unpaid full-time job, carrying no salary and created in the light of another's life work, work from which as a woman she would be excluded anyway, is no easy matter to justify, and in the 1980s would seem quite impossible to rationalize. The history and nature of priesthood – and we do take it seriously – as more than a job, mean that the dilemmas of the clergy wife cannot fairly be compared with those of other 'company wives'. Clergy wives should be forgiven for what sometimes looks like pompous demand for special regard.[4]

Above and beyond all the factors that make clergy wives a special case, there is the troubling fact that no other group of wives has to contend with: many people challenge the very existence of the clergy wife. The question of clerical celibacy is still being debated in the Roman Catholic Church, and the arguments used have remained largely unchanged since the Reformation. Or, to put it another way, the priest is the only figure in our culture whose right to marry has ever been questioned. The wife of a priest has to contend with a great deal: a high level of expectation in the context of traditional parish life on the one hand, and on the other a good many searching questions from feminist/modernist thought which challenges both the validity of these patterns and the concept of traditional marriage itself. Over and above these quandaries is the deeper need for justification, the need to prove that she is not a hindrance, and has a right to be in the vicarage in the first place! It would be a distortion to suggest that anybody would be so over-sensitive as to feel all these tensions at once (or would it?); but there is much evidence to suggest that more nail-biting agonizing over role and status occurs in this group of wives than in many others.

Here the historical perspective on celibacy is of interest. Obligatory clerical celibacy crept gradually upon Western Christendom. The earliest canonical enactment was Canon 33 of the Council of Elvira in the early fourth century. Papal decrees in 383 and 402 ordered celibacy for priests and Levites and later extended even to sub-deacons. Many priests came to ordination as married men, and Pope Leo the Great forbade the higher clergy to put away their wives, but enjoined them to continue living together as brother and sister. This bizarre arrangement caused administrative (to say

nothing of human) difficulties, and it was not long before the
Gallican Councils permitted ordination to married men only if
both husband and wife made vows of continence. By the eleventh
century – much later than popularly imagined – vows of perfect
chastity were required of priests and deacons. Eastern priests resisted more strenuously the pressures to give up their wives, and
the legal Orthodox position has always been the same: priests and
deacons may marry before ordination, but not after. Bishops,
drawn from the monastic tradition, remained celibate.[5]

Fleshly love and human parenthood were denied to those men
who had virtually exclusive guardianship of both theology and
sacrament. The redemptive power of sexual love found no place in
the poetry and piety of the church for centuries. This absence both
reflected and contributed to the monolithic clerical misogyny which
dominated Christian theology for centuries, and which somehow
managed to incorporate (and often ignore) the Christian gospel
insistence on the spiritual equality of men and women. This particular piece of co-existence depended upon a conception of female
spirituality as being more fleshly, more earthbound. 'Have not
women this renewal of the mind in which is the image of God?
Who would say this? But in the sex of their body they do not
signify this; therefore they are bidden to be veiled. The part,
namely, which they signify in the very fact of their being women,
is that which may be called the concupiscential part.'[6] So spoke
Augustine in the fifth century.

Tracing the philosophical and historical strands in Hellenic, Hebrew and provincial Roman culture which imposed their precon-
ceptions on the thinking of young churches is a fruitful area of
scholarship. The thinking that inspired St Paul and the early Fathers, and which came to shape mainstream theology, was limited
by all these considerations, and by the subsequent cultures the new
theology could be expressed in. It is not the task of this book to
do any more than point to work being done in this field. What we
do assert here is that the giant thinkers of the early church have a
greater chance of retaining their pride of place in Christian culture
through being opened up to present and future criticism and interpretation. The onus is on those who continue to defend the
'separate but equal' role of women on the grounds of tradition to
tell *us* just how much of that tradition we are supposed to respect.

On 29 April 1979, a group of women held a service at St
Botolph's Church in East London. We had gathered to celebrate
the ministry and personhood of women as part of a spiritual

first-aid programme following the synod defeat. Sayings of Jerome, Augustine, Tertullian and Chrystostom were written on large white banners and, as part of the liturgy, torn in two as a symbolic gesture. A retrospective glance makes us wish we had made them into confetti, blown our noses on them, or in some way treated the occasion with greater humour, less dourness. In case the reader has not heard before the well-worn list, here is a brief selection of 'oldies but baddies':

Nothing for men is shameful, for man is endowed with reason; but for woman it brings shame even to reflect on what her nature is (*Clement of Alexandria*).

The female sex is death's deaconess and is especially dishonoured of God (*Clement of Alexandria*).

Woman is a temple built over a sewer (*Jerome*).

It was necessary for woman to be made, as the scripture says, as a helper to man; not indeed, as a helpmate in other works, as some say, since man can be more efficiently helped by another man in other works; but as a helper in the work of generation ... As regards the individual nature, woman is defective and misbegotten (*St Thomas Aquinas*).

Women are gentle creatures in whose delicate hands God seems to have entrusted the future of the world in great part, as man's helper (Pope Pius XII).

Polemic against women did not miraculously stop when the Renaissance and Reformation began to shed their light on the church and world. A rearguard action was fought (mainly in Latin) and maintained for centuries. But the power of clerical hostility to women was gradually eroded as new voices were heard in the land. The humanists and love poets, the reformers and scientists, began to speak up in defence of women, paving the way to release from feudal constraint. It seemed that a new conception of woman's status and function was inevitable amidst such a dramatic shift of consciousness and values, swelling with the energy of the new, and feeding on the feudal patterns which were dying.

The advance of literacy and printing; the spirit of learning; the discovery of old worlds and new in the unearthing of classical works; the exploration of the seas; all contributed to the confidence and ebullience of 'Renaissance Man'. During the late Middle Ages, the new humanist consciousness of European thinkers initiated a debate and a controversy that was to last nigh on three centuries. *La Querelle des Femmes* – the dispute about women – was by and large a demand for women's education and a defence of intellectual equality. Our own St Thomas More championed the cause in England, and Erasmus lent his weight across the Channel. However posturing their debating tactics, however limited the long term benefits, the victory of their cause was a major triumph at the time.[7] The privileges of the court lady were no new-fangled egalitarian notion. Her elevation had its roots in the passionate, ritualistic lyrics of the troubadours of the princely courts in the more refined south of France and in Italy. Although essentially anti-social and adulterous, the cult of Lady worship was elevated and expressed with religious fervour. The advent of printing spread the fables of Provencal minstrelsy far beyond the hothouse world of court and castle which cradled them.

The Reformers thundered at all the above 'debauchery' as reformers do today; they were concerned with blowing 'fresh air into the cattle-shed of marital theory'.[8] In the north, where the Channel and iron-clad feudalism had until then kept southern voluptuousness at a distance, the Reformer's response to the decadence of the Old Church was to turn away from the convent ideal of virginity and to exalt the godliness of human love and marriage. Repugnance and high-minded puritanism, combined in this country with growing nationalism, and ultimately with national interest in the matrimonial dilemmas of Henry VIII, broke the monopoly of the Roman Catholic church.

The ensuing religious turmoil would take volumes of description, and there were times when both the Church of England itself and the marriage of its priests were considered dubious and probably short-lived benefits. The clergy wife, symbol and often orphan of the storms that followed, was born in the year 1549. Reader, we married him! So did Mrs Luther, and poor Mrs Cranmer could crawl out of the cupboard. (She had to crawl back in again when Queen Mary persecuted the reforming clergy of the new church.) Even the great Queen Elizabeth, considered by many to be a 'closet' Catholic, felt that married priesthood was more a symbol of decadence than of a brave new world. Her greeting to Mrs Parker, wife of the Archbishop of Canterbury, is memorable both for its direct and imperious language and its epitomizing the enigmatic status of the 'prieste's woman': 'Madame I may not call you, Mistress I am ashamed to call you, and so I do not know what to call you; but howsoever I thank you.'[9] Some historians believe it

was the precarious acceptance of their own unions that caused
Reformation clergy to extol the virtues of marriage and to raise its
spiritual status to such heights.

There is no doubt that an air of bravado characterized clergy
marriages in those early days. Sixteenth- and seventeenth-century
women were loved and celebrated in some of our language's most
amazing poetry. It was as if a dam had burst and the language of
God-love and woman-love could flow into and enrich each other.
We know from the life of a figure like John Donne just how hard
it was for him to confine his earthy spirituality and his soldier's,
courtier's and lover's wit into the parsonical strait-jacket of Anglican orders. When one's eyes are dazzled and blinded, it is quite
difficult to see limitations in Reformation theology of women.

So what happened? How did those brave pioneers settle down
to life in the claustrophobic close of the cathedral at Barchester, or
to the harsh, brooding monotony of Haworth? In the last chapter
we spoke of the professionalizing of holy orders. The rich diversity
of God's priestly army was lost when its more maverick and monk-
ish guerrillas were disbanded and sent back to their villages – or
into the flames and the dungeons. Those who were left, though not
automatically more worldly than the peasant army which preceded
them, had to learn diplomacy and survival in those troubled times.
All this contributed to a full-time, largely middle-class clerisy. But
that was not the only aspect of the Reformation which prevented
Christian *women* from achieving a long overdue restoration to
spiritual and social equality.

In our own day both feminist thought and mainstream theological exploration have sought out and defined the myopia of Reformation theology and the legacy inherited in the church today
from its blind spots, particularly in terms of the troubled 'woman
question'.[10] Reformation return to the Bible did nothing to resolve
the dualism inherent in church tradition, but was a return to a
different *sort* of sexism: not the staggering misogyny built up by
hundreds of years of patristic power, but the sexism implicit in
biblical patriarchy itself. Luther and Calvin emphasized again and
again the 'proper' function of women. Luther is to be cheered for
his cherishing of monogamous marriage and for his lively sideswipes at the body hatred accompanying the celibate ideal. 'That
godless knave,' he said about the Bishop of Mainz, 'forgetful of
his mother and sister, dares to blaspheme God's creature through
whom he himself was born.'[11] However robust his defence of
sexual love, Luther did not in essence depart from the Old Testa-

ment ethic of 'Daddy rules', or from the Pauline view of marriage as a hedge against lust. 'Women ought to stay at home – the way they were created indicates this, for they have broad hips and a wide fundament to sit upon, keep house and bear and raise children.'[12] The more austere Calvin emphasized the 'society, help and comfort' side of marriage; woman's purpose to 'help him (man) live more comfortably'. The change brought about by the Fall, he believed, moved woman not from freedom to subservience, but from subservience to slavery. All Christian women, regardless of marital status, were subject to male control, and in Calvin's Geneva an unfaithful wife merited the death penalty. His theology drew heavily from the authority of the church Fathers:

> The custom of the church, before Augustine was born, may be elicited first of all from Tertullian, who held that no woman in church is allowed to teach, speak, baptize or make offerings; this in order that she may not usurp the function of men, let alone those of priests. It is a mockery to allow women to baptize. Even the Virgin Mary was not allowed this.[13]

The female good life is circumscribed by married respectability. In a clerically-dominated church, the wife of the priest becomes a focus of this. She is the domesticated version of the 'souped-up Christian' syndrome. Ironically, the demotion of virginity and the religious life was part and parcel of her advent as well as her circumscription. Rosemary Radford Ruether describes the paradox:

> Protestantism contains the same basic theological roots of this patriarchal concept of the feminine. It too sanctions the feminine image of the church in relation to God the Father and the laity in relation to the father-clergy, in reciprocal relation to the proper submission of the wife to the husband. Indeed, the elimination of virginity as a role for women in the church also removed a sphere of female autonomy for women in the church of the Catholic tradition, leaving only the wife as role model for women ... The autonomous virgin with her ambivalent possibilities is dismissed, leaving only the silent, invisible pastor's wife as a model for the good Christian woman.[14]

Silent and invisible we are not! We must, though, attempt to describe the many ways our dubiously accorded status has separated us, and the loyal, gentle women of our own communion, from the fray of subsequent revolution and feminist awareness. The early days were precarious despite the courageous consciousness of the age. If Mrs Cranmer had to spend her life hidden in a box drilled with air holes, it is perhaps not surprising that many of her descendent sisters have settled happily for a parsonage and a steady income! The exigencies of the Civil War, and the ups and downs of Popery and Puritanism of the Caroline and Jacobean ages, made many a gentle and unworldly clergy family fall on evil days. The wife of the ultra-Puritan minister may well have shared his martyrdoms: such hardships were by no means offset by the ideals of Commonwealth impinging on the family hearth. The poet Milton's 'He for God only, She for God in him' must have brought sparse comfort in times of persecution.

We owe an enormous debt to the sectarians for an improvement in women's theological status. From the seventeenth century onwards, it was these groups rather than the followers of the Reformation giants who tapped the rich resources of strength and piety in their female adherents. The Baptists and the Brownites had women preachers by the middle of the seventeenth century. Quakerism, the tradition most richly endowed with women saints, aimed at restoring the sexual equality of Paradise. Calvin's prohibition was levelled partly at the Anabaptists, who allowed women the function of baptism as early as the mid-sixteenth century.

Against this background there looms the darkest and most terrible of all women's suffering – the witch hunts. It may seem initially irrelevant or in bad taste to mention this in a 'civilized' discussion of hearth and home; but the connection between the two themes becomes clearer every time we take out the map of our past. Feminists have looked long and hard at this most ignominious piece of ecclesiastical history, and exposed the ruthless misogyny at the heart of its rationale and methods. The practice cannot be dismissed simply as mediaeval bloodthirstiness and superstition. Indeed, the most vociferous opponents of witch hunts amongst the church hierarchy (Charlemagne, Rabanus Maurus, Pope Gregory VII, for example) were in power during the period of history we term the Middle (or Dark) Age! Witch hunting reached its most lethal level of efficiency at the very time women were being restored to 'wedded godliness'. A grim irony, that the era of history termed 'Renaissance' and 'Reformation' is the time when hundreds of thousands, perhaps millions, of women were executed for 'crimes' more closely allied to healing, midwifery and a knowledge of folklore than to any satanic influence.

When John Robinson touched so slightly on this theme (see the quotation at the beginning of this chapter), he hinted that there were indeed women who may not have been happy to have either their social or spiritual status subsumed and justified by patriarchal protection. Conventional 'wisdom' has always assumed that women who were not chosen in marriage were either recalcitrant scolds or simply unendowed with the necessary attractions. But in time of spiritual fanaticism pity and scorn are compounded by fear. *Witch*! The name and punishment were given to multitudes of women whose only crime was that they were free of the dead hand of male control. 'When a woman thinks alone, she thinks evil', says the *Malleus Maleficarum* of Jacobus Sprenger.[15] Persecution of witches was even more pitiless under the Puritans of seventeenth-century England. Ecclesiastical suspicion of 'untamed' female creativity has not always been so dramatically assuaged, but with the convent door closed to all but devout followers of the Old Church, home and hearth became almost exclusively the right and proper place for female spiritual destiny to be contained and expressed acceptably. Formal priesthood having cornered the market on institutionalized holy living, the clergy wife became the mirror and paradigm of *womanly* holy living. The story of the path from theology to social reality can be traced in the vivid pictures of social and parish life that we can read and enjoy in Post-Reformation literature. The only clear social record of parson's wife and 'other women' is in the letters and literature of this time. The road from Mrs Cranmer to our troubled sisters in the church today opens up on many a colourful landscape, peopled by both dragons and damsels in distress, gentle Amelias and fearsome Mrs Proudies. The English novel sheds a far more searching light on this theme than any amount of arid theorizing or puzzled contemplation of those faded sepia photographs which hang in our vestries and vicarages.

By the time the novel emerged as a major form of social description, most of the dust of old battles had blown away and we begin to see the settled realities of parish life in an easy co-existence of church and state. In the early episodic tales of Fielding, Richardson and their ilk in the eighteenth century, the clergyman and his family are part of a tapestry of saints and sinners. The ladies of those early portraits have the roughness and ribaldry of their author's tales as well as their author's time upon them. But the pervading message of the Reformers is still to be discerned amidst the Hogarth-like liveliness. Once wooed and won – however heartily – the good wife must be practical and capable as well as loving if wedded bliss is to be consolidated into honourable marriage. The message is relayed, underlined and in block capitals in the case of the wife of the Good Parson. Mrs Adams, in Fielding's *Joseph Andrews*, is the practical bedrock of her husband's quixotic saint-liness. She is as good as the earth – warm and loyal. We love her, and so does Parson Adams. So what's the problem?

The problem in part is this. If the good wife refuses the part of Martha and seeks a strange destiny of her own, she threatens both the honour and the heroic stature of her husband. Even in our own time we have not yet managed to shake off this idea. Who can put hand on heart and say that he does not – if only slightly – pity a William Godwin, a George Henry Lewes or a Leonard Woolf?[16] Why do clergy wives feel that these tensions remain writ so large in their own lives? Is it that the wives of other men are in fact freer to change the script and the rules? When Mrs Hook wrote her article in 1976, she exhibited temerity in listing the qualities necess-ary for the clergy wife in International Woman's Year: '. . . the hoped-for presence in the rectory, ideally the sympathizer, the provider of resources, the link person as well as the agent respon-sible for ensuring that her husband is freed from emotional worries of his own . . . the multifarious time-consuming chores that will help make her husband's show a good one.' The really unaccept-able face of Mrs Hook's message (and she is surely aware of this herself) is not simply that her list may well have served for Mrs Adams, but that it does not take the intervening centuries into account; such an observation is in itself depressing. According to Mrs Hook, a failure to comply with her requirements will endanger not only domestic and social harmony, but the *spiritual viability* of a priestly ministry which will take its toll in the community if undermined: 'If the clergy wife submerges her desire for personal fulfilment in the multifarious time-consuming chores that will help make her husband's show a good one, what she does out of sup-portive love for her husband has love of God and love of neighbour as an end-product.'[17]

If this basic prescription has not altered much down the centu-ries, some of the 'multifarious chores' have undergone some radical surgery. If a parson is poor, the good sense, industry and thrift of his wife will not only enhance his pastoral prowess; they will keep him respectably above the poverty line and out of the debtor's prison. If he is well-to-do, then wifely virtue can be safely embel-lished with graciousness and beauty, while servants take over the soup kitchen.

Graciousness was indeed the order of the day in the world of Jane Austen. The country wives gave way to their more sophisticated sisters who decorated the parsonages that belonged, by right, to those connected to it by birth or privilege. Miss Austen's novels contain no analysis of 'Age of Reason' spirituality, but there is wealth enough of other wonders to give their author pride of place in the literature of clerical life. The rectory and its inhabitants are, as today, of major importance in the settled life of the small village depicted so perfectly by Miss Austen. They are part of the star cast rather than supporting actors of earlier literature, and they are certainly portrayed in all their shame, sham and glory. The six novels give us an irreplaceable description of the ease and gentility of their age.

How much of the clergy-wife stereotype do we owe to the larger-than-life characters in *Mansfield Park* and *Emma*? As we labour under the archaic but persistent expectations which burden many of us today, we find in Jane Austen an easy target for our protestations and embarrassment. She showed the world a gentle, easy life lived in gracious houses, a world where the parsonage was second in importance only to the Big House; and the occupants of both were each others' natural companions. The Crawfords were daily visitors to the Bertrams of *Mansfield Park*. Indeed, life at the Park was deemed so dull by the Bertrams while the vicarage was empty that the reader might imagine the surrounding dwellings deserted! In *Pride and Prejudice*, the visits that poor Charlotte Collins had to endure from her illustrious patroness, the odious Lady Catherine de Bourgh, were indispensable to her toadying husband. *Emma*'s Mr Elton, 'a very pretty young man and a very proper vicar of Highbury', regarded Hartfield as his second home and its mistress as a fitting wife, until the even more snobbish Emma pointed out the proper limits of squirearchy by arranging a more humble marriage for him.

'No! No!' we cry, 'it's not like that any more.' But our protestations are muffled by the fact that many clergy wives still live in those houses, especially in the country. A substantial number of clergy are still uneasy at being cut off from their middle-class counterparts in difficult parish situations. Modern ecclesiastical jargon names this tension 'lack of leadership support', and it is often a very real difficulty when accompanied by inner-city decay and ghettoism. But the 'us-ish-ness' about it is a necessary observation.

Jane Austen's works are often held up by critics of the church to expose and mock its worldliness, and are only enjoyed by the present-day faithful with a somewhat uneasy laughter. Her unique description of clerical life lies in her total absence of social critique. With irony and with devastating wit, she aimed at the vanity and pretensions of individual men and women. Her villain is not the church itself, but those who succumb to its limitations. Her barbs are reserved for snobbery and mercenary compromise. Unable to reach the Grange Heights of her more decorative sister, 'Miss Ward found herself obliged to be attached to the Rev. Mr Norris.' It is easy to forget Jane Austen's gentle admiration for those who negotiate the labyrinths of connection, preferment and intrigue to emerge into the fresh air of vocation and goodness. Her novels depict, through drawing room dramas of who-marries-who, the wider moral dilemmas of clerical and social life. Unfortunately, moral rectitude and good sense are not to be enlivened by wit, brilliance or irreverence in the case of the parson's marriage. No Elizabeth Bennetts in the Rectory! In *Mansfield Park*, Edmund Bertram's vocation is preserved by the banishment of the mocking Mary Crawford and his union with the virtuous but – alas! – rather dull Fanny Price. The message of the Reformers and Mrs Hook prevails now, in Jilly Cooper's memorable phrase, 'sicklied o'er with the pale thought of caste'. If *he* is to be free in order to be truly 'spiritual', she must be not just a godly matron but a rather sober one! The qualities that preserve the honour of the church in parishes up and down the land must be enshrined in the clergy wife's daily life for her husband to be able to soar beyond propriety to higher things and greater mercies. They remain the same to this day – a practical (but not *too* worldly) approach to material prosperity, industry and good-heartedness.

Jane Austen tells only the story of the rural gentility she knew so intimately. For the challenges of the wider world of industrial town and disenfranchised poor, we turn to the writing of George Eliot and to the life *and* work of Mrs Gaskell and the Brontës. From these authors, depicting nineteenth-century life in the North and Midlands, there emerges a different kind of woman. As befits the earnestness of the age, she is more utilitarian and more dedicated to duty; this because she experiences at first hand the grinding poverty of wage labour. The clergy themselves are more solemn and less aristocratic, and the age of the large family has arrived. The 'multifarious chores' assumed terrifying proportions. In George Eliot's *Scenes of Clerical Life*, the saintly Amelia Barton is harried by the endless demands of parish and home life, and by the struggle to make ends meet without capital wealth. She does her mending secretly in the night so that none shall know of her lonely unaided labours. She succumbs in the end to death in child-birth. The preceding century's legacy was a clerical image of easy gentility which compounded the struggles of those unable to sustain it. Milly Barton, like her real-life contemporaries the Brontë sisters, was patronized and pitied by the idle women of means and alien-ated by her 'position' from the camaraderie of other poor women. The shadowy world of the governess, documented so memorably in Charlotte Brontë's *Jane Eyre*, was the fate of legions of poor clergy daughters. Educated for useful service, they lived a silent shadowy life, marooned on the stairs between the servants' hall and the bright lights of the drawing room. Marriage was the only hope of rescue . . .

Charlotte Brontë was vilified by the ecclesiastical establishment of her day for portraying the plight of women under Victorian patriarchy with such passionate anger. The autonomous woman was effectively killed off in the dominant literature of the Victorian era; there is a plethora of loyal literature on the theme of the happy parsonage with mother and father giving a fine example of trad-itional piety to brilliant sons and accomplished daughters. Great happiness and great sanctity there undoubtedly was. Dedication of so many lives to the poor could not, however, offset the alienating and omnipresent image of gentility and the fact of establishment. It was in many communities the earthy vigour of the new Meth-odism which breathed new life into the mission field of industrial-ized England. The impact of this reforming sect is a major theme in two of George Eliot's most important novels, *Middlemarch* and *Adam Bede*. In Adam Bede, the benign presence of Mr Irwine, the gentleman parson, is confined to his elegant 'olde worlde' setting of church and vicarage. The heroine of the book is Dinah Morris, an itinerant gospel preacher who gathers the poor about her in the open air, helps the poor women in their kitchens, and comforts the widow's distress by sharing her humble bed for the night.

The shadow fell early on the spirited preaching of Dinah Morris. The Methodists, like the Reformers before them, while questioning the church's easy co-existence with materialism and secular values, did not question the paternalism at the root of the problem. The Methodist Conference bowed to convention and forbade women to preach. Dinah had to exercise her ministry from the heart of home and family. Another important safety valve of female auton-

omy, part of the more varied possibilities for women in the eighteenth century, was sealed off.

The Victorians deified female subservience into the 'Angel in the
House'. Any lingering wifely envy and suspicion of independent
female achievement was hardened into piteous scorn. The ascendance of cherished wife over career woman was now total. In our
own time, feminists and others are aware that these old divisions
still apply, consciously or unconsciously, to women. In the church
this phenomenon is more tenaciously maintained to this day than
it is in the 'secular' world, an inevitable consequence, since professional doors in secular life are continuing to open while those of
the church remain closed. The rights and wrongs of this aside, it
is certainly true that the newly reborn independent woman feels
ill-at-ease in the church today, especially if she is single. Her sister
outside is spiritually freed from the fetters of male theology, and
more and more likely to heap the scorn, which once fell on her,
upon the traditional wife – especially the vicar's![18]

Those who by choice or necessity justify their traditional married
life-style, and clergy wives loom large in this group, often sigh for
the good old days when role and status were secure. 'The clergy
wife, having lost her previous status, is somewhat excluded from
the structure of the church and often feels unsupported.'[19] She
always was excluded from the structure, of course, but considerable
status has in the past masked this unpalatable fact. Witness the
posh ladies of Trollope's *Barchester Towers*:

> The Archdeacon's wife, in her happy home at Plumpstead,
> knows how to assume the full privileges of her rank, and ex-
> presses her own mind in becoming tone and place. But Mrs
> Grantly's sway, if sway she has, is easy and beneficent. She never
> shames her husband: before the world she is a pattern of obe-
> dience; her voice is never loud, nor her looks sharp: doubtless,
> she values power and has not unsuccessfully striven to acquire
> it: but she knows what should be the limit of a woman's rule.[20]

The ominous beginning of Trollope's very next paragraph indicates
the danger of vicarious status: 'Not so Mrs Proudie . . .', introduc-
ing one of the most monstrous and memorable of our kind in all
fiction. Mrs Proudie enjoys wider fame than any real-life counterpart. She is rightly vilified for wielding her power so mercilessly;
often she is used as an argument for clerical celibacy! But the real
offensiveness of Mrs Proudie's machinations is that they are conducted not from her individual self-respect and responsibility, but

from a dubiously bargained second-hand power. She's really a Mrs Grantly with the gloves off, who has thrown away the clerical Queensbury Rules! Feminist thinkers have pointed out that there is a bribe to which many women succumb in traditional marriage: that of enjoying a man's power vicariously; praised and patronized by him as right hand, while enjoying immunity from the risks he must take.

How much has this false picture of domestic virtue, painted by the Mrs Proudies of our world, contributed to the lessening of other people outside the magic circle of her approval, with her bullying and her games of 'company wives'?

In the wider world today, the power games of the company wife are increasingly irrelevant and ignored with ease. With autonomous women moving into key positions of responsibility, there is new potential for mutuality and support to develop, with couples supporting each other's contributions to the world outside the home. The fragile and private nature of traditional wifely authority is recognized for what it is. Within parish life, the subsidiary roles undertaken by clergy wives and loyal laywomen preserve the ethos of traditional marriage *per se*, as a microcosm of the relations between men and women in the Christian community. Church women's isolation from feminist awareness is increased by the continuing isolation of the church itself. From the nineteenth century onwards, the church has experienced a loss of power and become the 'dependent powerless sanctifier of nostalgic domesticity'.[21] The beleaguered clergy wife has found her traditional role both undervalued yet simultaneously stubbornly assumed. Nostalgia for some sort of kudos becomes more understandable when one considers the kind of tasks assigned to the unpaid employee (read clergy wife) of a powerless pacifier (read clergyman).

The dilemmas of the present-day clergy wife are real, and feminist thought, while making no claim to hold all the answers, has something to contribute. It is appropriate to outline what the specific problems are for the wives of 1980. Our own recent times have added burdens other than those already mentioned, and at first glance it could easily seem as if the women's liberation movement has exacerbated rather than clarified the problem. The need for mutual fulfilment in marriage is often simplified, by those in and out of the church, into controversy about wives working outside the home. For most women, of course, the choice has not existed, since home-based work all but vanished during the Industrial Revolution. It is fast disappearing, through present economic

stress, for the wives of priests, who moreover will most likely have
skills and training which necessitate a formal sphere of exercise.
The combination of traditional expectation and economic necessity
lays bare an important area of Anglican hypocrisy. As we have
seen, most Anglican clergymen came from the upper or middle
classes, and their comforts or lack of them depended on private
means. In past times a poor parson's wife was unlikely to be able
to mitigate financial distress by any other means than stringent
economic management. Even in the very recent past, this fact has
affected clergy deployment in a very real way. Standardization of
clergy pay is a recent innovation; among our friends there are both
those whose work is only possible by either a wife's earnings or a
family inheritance and those who are unable to take on vital areas
of work because neither of these sources is available to them – e.g.,
bachelors and fathers of very young families. Nevertheless, many
communities still cling to the concept of 'two-for-the-price-of-one'.
This concept is both inhibiting and dishonest when centred on the
clergy family and assumptions of long-vanished prosperity, in spite
of its connection to a long tradition of voluntary work, pioneered
by the church, and nourished by its largely middle-class clientèle.
To what extent the role of ancillary wife is still expected or adhered
to is a question fraught with ambiguity for the women concerned,
and with euphemistic posturing on the part of those with a vested
interest in the status quo. The latter group may well afford to be
euphemistic, but the ancillary wife bears the reality.

In her survey, Janet Spedding found that stereotype and reality
matched. She originally set out to investigate how and why such
a stereotype, i.e., one made in the light of somebody else's occupation, could exist in the 1970s, when women's own independent
work is the nearly universal given among the young and middle
class. (Her interviewees were both predominantly young and middle class.) They were to a woman not much touched by the phenomenon of the women's movement in the set-up of the clergy
marriage; it was by no means assumed in this group that working
as one's husband's ancillary is a 'sin' of the past. All of the women
made substantial traditional contributions to their husband's work:
teaching in Sunday school, taking women's groups (over which
most assumed formal or informal leadership), tasks concerned with
the upkeep of the church, i.e., flowers and cleaning, receptionist
work based in the home such as answering the door and taking
messages. The work was generally judged by the women concerned
to be time-consuming to the point of necessitating that their own

personal interests be put in the background or abandoned. Dedication and patience appear to be the keynote, as well as a level of purely domestic activity that would be considered unacceptable by most of the women's own contemporaries.[22] Of course there are variations in the pattern, relating to both the age of the woman herself, the number and age of her children and denominational affiliation. But the life patterns reflected most strongly the phenomena we discussed in chapter 5; that the sexual polarization of work-roles is both conservative and unimaginative in parish life. There are obviously many exceptions, and it is important to remember that the women Janet Spedding interviewed were all drawn from one area of the country. The fact that the exceptions still elicit comment or congratulation speaks for itself. An enlightened clergyman of our acquaintance once told us proudly that his new job freed his wife from having to do sixty choir teas a week. 'Have to' are words not entirely unknown even here in enlightened NW3 and beleaguered E14; experience has shown us that traditional expectations are a dramatic reality whether they are met or resisted.

Some serious questions are in order: to what extent do clergy and laity alike make parochially expedient exceptions of principle in the case of 'women's work'? If the guide-lines of the gospel parable of the talents are ignored and work distributed on the basis of custom and convenience, does that work still have authentic value? How far do congregations, to talk in specifics, expect the clergy wife to be an unpaid curate? If they do have such expectations, who, in our day, is prepared to defend them as legitimate? The answer is that congregations really do have the expectations but do not like to say so. This anomaly is rooted in the status quo of sexual apartheid of church communities. To the above we must add the phenomenon of clericalism itself, as well as traditional views of marriage and the 'separate but equal' role of women strongly upheld by church people and defended by influential groups like the Mothers' Union. This combination of circumstances makes it hard for clergy families and congregations to shake off stifling assumptions about their lives. In the Christian context, tasks performed entirely from duty are best left undone – or at best make the recipients uncomfortable! Labourers are worthy of their hire and clergy wives are in a bind. Largely set apart from feminist awareness, they are nonetheless part of the historical process – on the defensive yet again.

Although no feminist would have any truck with the 'You spiritual – Me Useful' symbiosis of traditional clerical marriage, or with any kind of elevation of wifehood into status-seeking masked as humility, we do not make a god either of the 9-to-5 day or the privacy of the nuclear family. Many see and explain the problem solely in these terms: 'You poor dear, having folk in and out all day' but for many home-based women the troupe of visitors is a major joy.

The open-house tradition is perhaps the most admirable aspect of clerical life today. Freed from patriarchy and clericalism, its possibilities are enormous. The healthy society of the future – the dream of feminist utopia – is one in which the barriers between working and being are blurred, if not broken. Priesthood at its best is primarily about grace, about being and availability rather than function. An open vicarage can be the place where that dream is realized and begins to make sense beyond itself in the wider community. When the Christian community lives in an open, sharing way (and in rare and wonderful places it does begin to live thus), it can challenge the introverted chauvinism of the nuclear family as the gospel demands.

Feminist activity is commonly understood to aim for the inclusion of all women in the work force and to be dedicated to the euthanasia of monogamous marriage. Not true. The women's movement is looking towards the wider dream of fuller citizenship for women in a world which recognizes them as the full equals of men. They would not look askance at the Christian communities who are experimenting with the New Testament ideals of pooled resources, home-based shared work, egalitarian decision-making – all of which tend to negate the perverted idea that home-based work is peripheral. In urban life, the traditional vicarage is one of the rare places where the home can be more than a private haven or box. The possibilities offered by her unique situation will bear on the clergy wife's decision about where to use her energies. A decision to stay around and help her husband need not in her case mean a withdrawal from public activity (women with children opt to work outside the home despite the difficulties because they need the money and because the real world is 'out there'). If she stays at home she will certainly meet with a good deal of approval, and not just from those who would see her kept as a menial chained to the chutney. Their approval is easily dispensed with except by the most querulous; but what about those in need, who deeply appreciate her ministrations? The clergy wife who knows she is at home because it is where she *chooses* to be has in that choice a great and deep strength.

Because the traditional role does offer liberating possibilities, many wives are anxious about rejecting it. Many, though, find the demands so devouring and domestic that they take the only way out and deny the existence of any role at all. This solution is often tragic for the woman concerned, for she can be constrained to deny a loving and lively interest in her husband's life in a desperate effort to preserve the autonomy of her own. A false view of marriage as an area of 'private life' is neither feminist nor Christian, and is certainly not conducive to love, mutuality or human happiness. The demands of love and justice are pinpointed in an almost nightmarish way in the clergy wife's situation. It is a shaky and dualistic theology that would separate these demands, and there is some evidence that the chickens of Reformation double-think are coming home to roost. We are no longer immune in our respectability.

Several of our clergy friends are involved in the present debate about the re-marriage of divorced people in church. This subject is fraught and difficult, and too complex to go into here. But there is a great fear, which we are told informs these deliberations, that if divorce and re-marriage were made 'respectable' by a liberalizing of church law, many clergy couples would openly admit failure and throw in the towel. In a clericalized church, widespread clergy divorce would bring chaos and many doubt if the centre could hold.

Rescue will come from nothing less than a reappraisal of Christian ministry and Christian marriage. The church, that sleeping giant, needs to awake and throw off some of the chains with which it has shackled both its women and its ministry. A new Reformation theology of women would be a good place to begin. A return to that sound Reformation principle of the priesthood of all believers is long overdue. True laicization and – dare we say it – whole priesthood would enable the vicar's wife and her lay sisters to make, not nonsense of Women's Lib, but a good deal more Christian sense.

Present developments in the church are ensuring that male/female, lay/clerical patterns of work are reinforced. Women who remain active in such a church will be those who either seek to appease or to emulate male power patterns. If the church does not recognize and bless the new vision of many of its women, if it closes the parsonage door and seeks the solace of the sweet, familiar face by the fireside, it will find she has either fallen asleep or gone to join the monstrous regiment who are breaking down the gate.

7

Sisters of Cassandra

'Wisdom cries aloud in the street;
In the markets she raises her voice;
On the tops of the walls
She cries out;
At the entrance of the city gates
She speaks . . .'(Proverbs 1.20f.).

'I know that the rest of my life will be spent working for transformations I shall not live to see realized. I feel daily, hourly impatience and am pledged to the active and tenacious patience that a lifetime commitment requires: there can be no resignation in the face of backlash, setback or temporary defeat: there can be no limits on what we allow ourselves to imagine. Because the past ten years of feminist thinking and action have been so full, so charged with revelation, challenges as well as anger and pain, we sometimes think of that decade as if it had been fifty years and not ten. *Why haven't we come further?* But in the great evolution of women this century's radical feminism envisions, we have only begun. And yet this longer historical view seems unbearable to me when I consider that the urgency of each woman's life may be lost, poured away like dishwater, because history does not move fast enough for her' (Adrienne Rich, *On Lies, Secrets and Silences*).

'And though the last lights off the black west went
Oh, morning, at the brown brink eastward, springs –
Because the Holy Ghost over the bent
World broods with warm breast and with Ah!
  Bright wings' (Gerard Manley Hopkins).

*   *   *

In writing this book we find ourselves continuing to debate the importance of the symbol of female priesthood in the healing role of the church. We began with a question – 'Why?' Why is the church the last place to initiate the true feminization of the moral order enshrined in its gospel? Why is the church the last place to make the equality of men and women a reality in its structures? In pursuing these questions we have set for ourselves a heavy and continuing task. The journey has led us to great minds, poetry and possibilities. It has led us, in our reading and understanding of women's history and women's thoughts, to strange places where our own experiences have seemed pale shadows of the hopes and pains of some of our sisters – pain so searing that we, borne up by privilege and healthy egotism, can only begin to comprehend. The issue of women's ordination seems very far away, and it is hard to remember that such a parochial symbol is where we are called to nail our colours to the mast. To claim a substantial historical significance for 8 November 1978 seems so grandiose. Personal setbacks are common stuff in the political world of synod decisions, and the ecclesiastical deliberations that inspire books have about them a ring of far greater solemnity than the General Synod of the Church of England. But our work in 'secular' feminism reinforces a conviction that a yearning for spiritual dimension is as powerful amongst those who have rejected the church as in those who remain, and our vision of a shared priesthood springs from a fundamental certainty that a commitment to Christ's gospel is inseparable from liberationist struggle. In this sense, female priesthood is peripheral unless it revolutionizes the system, if those who offer it are proposing to be sucked into a structure that is caste-ridden, fearful and repressive. Why bother? Feminist thought and Christian feminist vision open up vistas of possibilities and urgent tasks quite apart from the *obvious* eye-sore of an all-male priesthood. It is easy, of course, to fall into the trap that women themselves have so often been the victims of – the dismissive, élitist and ultimately diminishing trap of saying, 'I've got better things to do than concern myself with your petty affairs.' Part of the purpose of this chapter is to show how destructive such a pose is in the nurturing of our children, our church and our earth. Feminist theology, indeed all theology at its best, gives us new models of thinking, new ways to describe our centres of gravity and grace and 'the ground of our beseeching'.[1] Thus we accept that the petty and parochial tasks that we struggle with every day are as import-ant as our prayers and dreams. We found this to be true at every stage of this book's creation. People are being damaged by uncertainty and schism, and so the seemingly archaic demands of the present campaign must be met.

Feminist thought, with its rediscovery and emphasis on the importance of symbol, has enhanced and reinforced for us the sacramental nature of Christian life and worship. We are therefore brought back to the reassessed but pre-eminent symbol of priesthood, as well as to the pinwheel symbol of our almost private language. If the pyramid were in any way still real to us (see chapter 4) we would long ago have left those Levites somewhere back in the tabernacle.

An understanding of history is essential for a working knowledge of the main strands of church history, and for an understanding of how that history relates to women's second-class citizenship. We realize that it would take our whole lives just getting our minds round the dynamics of female oppression and discovering women's hidden history. In this context, it is easy to bury oneself in this quest and thereby neglect the necessity to act on the present. But we see with great clarity that these tasks of patient scholarship must not be a substitute for acting on the present moment.

A national Movement for the Ordination of Women (MOW) has been set up; in connection with our particular research, letters from new friends are here before us, letters full of pain at the direction the church seems to be taking. The present paralysis and backlash (documented in chapter 5) is a good place to enter the struggle. At least it is home. It is a sobering thought that many radical women who continue in the institutional church often remain loyal because of a professional commitment or a good marriage. In marriage these women love one man so much that they could never, through all disillusion, abandon anything to which he has given his life. In any case, a beloved priest husband does not really belong to an organization, but to people. We count ourselves among this group, and we hope somehow to represent the many women who have left and to continue carrying the torch – affirming that there is the means of grace and the hope of glory in the church.

What can we say, after two thousand years, about the church's power to give and enshrine divine revelation, to hold God's loving purposes before men and women, when it has so often and so diabolically been mistaken? By today's standards, the religions' histories make them oppressors of women; they are traditions with a great deal of retribution to make, and we can only affirm that, while we make no claim to superiority, we are deeply committed to the task of healing.

Because we are Christian, we have begun to glimpse the genuine core of the faith, the divinity and amazing love of Christ. We are thus open to the message of the gospel, and we can sometimes begin to distinguish the message of the founder from some of the distortions of his followers. There is no man or message like Jesus. Dorothy L. Sayers put it this way in her essay 'Are Women Human?':

> Perhaps it is no wonder that the women were first at the cradle and last at the Cross. They had never known a man like this man – there never has been such another. A prophet and teacher who never nagged at them, never flattered or coaxed or patronized; who never made arch jokes about them, never treated them either as 'The women, God help us', or 'The ladies, God bless them', who rebuked without querulousness and praised without condescension, who took their questions and arguments seriously; who never mapped out their sphere for them, never urged them to be feminine or jeered at them for being female . . . There is no act, no sermon, no parable in the whole Gospel that borrows its pungency from female perversity; nobody could possibly guess from the words and deeds of Jesus that there was anything 'funny' about women's nature. But we might easily deduce it from his contemporaries, and from his prophets before him, and from his Church to this day. Women are not human.[2]

Our ultimate vision and description of a peaceable kingdom, a community free of sexism, contains nothing that is not at least glimpsed in the life of Jesus and in rare but wonderful words of the Old Testament prophets. We are talking about a world that has never yet existed. For our generation of Christian women, Jesus symbolizes our liberation as he has symbolized all human longing for justice; in the yearning songs of the slaves of every century and the liberation theology of our own era, a theology born in Brazilian shanties shadowed by Western wealth and prosperity. 'Love is all his meaning,' wrote Lady Julian of Norwich;[3] at times we realize that the body of Christ holds more in common with such visions as hers than any of our sectarian striving would ever lead us to imagine.

Every great movement for change has been accused by its detractors of tearing God from the heavens. The dismantling of patriarchy, probably the most radical step yet proposed to change human society, will not end the meaning and power of transcendence, because transcendence is not summed up in patriarchy. Instead, it has led the faithful to reassess where indeed God does reign and rest. This in spite of the fact that many feminists claim patriarchy and concepts of divinity to be inseparable. 'Jesus Christ cannot symbolize the liberation of women. A culture that maintains a masculine image for its highest divinity cannot allow its women to experience themselves as the equals of men,' writes Naomi Goldenberg.[4]

In what sense does our culture maintain a masculine image for its divinity? To be sure, we use the masculine pronoun, and this deeply affects and limits our imagination[5] (as well, we hasten to add, as being a great offence to many women), but gospel and Pauline insistence on the spiritual equality of men and women is real enough and the generic bluff can be called at any time. Any chauvinistic pretensions to male supremacy, linguistic, liturgical or theological, to any God-deep significance of the male pronoun simply will not hold. Goldenberg talks of how we experience ourselves when smothered by male-created imagery. We are aware of this, and will continue to sharpen our awareness in order to synthesize our thoughts and nourish our spirits. Goldenberg's pursuit of the above theme leads her, at the end of her book,[6] to propose the celebration of female existential experience in a form of witchcraft. She has, it seems to us, been dangerously ensnared into distorting the importance of individual experience and thereby destroying its life-giving power. Belief in the resurrection ensures that individual reality does not end with earthly life. Asserting such faith should in no way cancel out the urgency of using *this* life to be acutely aware of the need for change *here and now* as an inseparable part of the salvation-eternity process.

Goldenberg's deification of personal experience too easily leads to a denial of the experience of others. What an insult her statement is to the male friends, brothers, husbands, lovers and fathers who share our struggles and fight for our liberation *and* theirs, who need to be joined to us. Experiencing ourselves as the equals of men is of little value if we cease to love them. From our own women's history of weakness and silence, from our untold stories, comes a critique of the church and the rediscovery of its purpose. This critique must never become a petulant whine of 'I don't want to play in your yard'.

The established church in particular (and organized religion in general) is so widely and deeply experienced as oppressive of human striving for justice that we who hold to the institution have real charges to answer. With this in mind, Christian Cassandras will want to ask, 'What irreplaceable resources – pearls of great price – are to be found in the worldly structures of organized religion?' If Christian practice is more than an expression of primitive fear and the need to appease the strange raging forces of the 'oblong blur'; if it is more than an attempt to mould the individual to dominant community practices and socially sanctioned decent behaviour',[7] we need to seek out and to describe these areas. If our faith is a real recognition and adoration of a loving God who creates us and wills our good, then the church of its founder is built, despite all error, to hallow all the human and natural world and to take it to perfection.

To begin our 'irreplaceable resources' test, we attempt to discover whether the Judaeo-Christian language of death and rebirth has any political reality in the healing of today's world. Can the church and faith of our fathers offer any new and powerful truth for the healing of patriarchy itself? Can it help us to die to all that is un-whole in a male-dominated church and world? Can it free us from the 'necessities' of male supremacy?

These men who have turned the world upside down have come here also . . . (Acts 17.6).

There have been some startling moments in the history of God's people when they have been called to bridge the chasm between the example of Jesus and the necessities of survival in a world of group interests. The history of the early church, as recorded in the book of Acts, relates the baptism of the Roman centurion Cornelius by Peter as such a moment. Hardly had the struggling young church begun to find its identity in a perilous and hostile world, when it was called to share the long-awaited fulfilment of God's covenant with the alien and enemy Gentile culture. The young church had to die to any pretensions of spiritual and racial supremacy almost before it had time to draw breath. From Peter's dream came the historical possibilities for growth: 'I was in the city of Joppa praying; and in a trance I saw a vision, something descending, like a great sheet, let down from heaven by four corners; and it came down to me. Looking at it closely I observed animals and beasts of prey and reptiles and birds of the air. And I heard a voice saying to me, "Rise, Peter; kill and eat." But I said, "No, Lord; for nothing common or unclean has ever entered my mouth." But the voice answered a second time from heaven, "What God has cleansed you must not call common" ... If then God gave the same gift to them as he gave to us when we believed in the Lord Jesus Christ, who was I that I could withstand God?' (Acts 11.5–17).

It would have been quite easy to stand in God's way today; Peter could have taken the matter to the General Synod. On a more serious note, if Peter had said 'no' to his vision, the new church would have remained a Jewish sect and none of us would know of it.

Post-biblical historical touchstones abound too. The courageous inspiration of the abolitionists was another great leap of faith. The Christians who helped initiate and bring about this great enterprise were part of a culture and indeed a religious climate which hallowed economic prosperity and expansion as divinely blessed. The impetus for freeing slaves, if not the actual enactment, came at a time when to do so was considered economically disastrous.

Biblical texts were used to defend slavery as well as other forms of racial supremacy, war and the 'proper' sphere of women – the list is endless. But the dominant theme of the gospels is an undeniable call to oppose the whole worldly notion that we should somehow strive for the survival of our way of life. Women of spirit are learning that gospel prohibition against exclusiveness must encompass the more immediate and parochial of our own feminist aims. The challenges of global injustice, a near toxic planet, and the prospect of nuclear annihilation ensure that feminist vision cannot end with a new deal from men. We must sustain nothing less than the hope that there is still time for a new covenant with the earth itself and the whole human family. We are being called again, as St Peter was, not to hug anything to ourselves, even our precious new-found sisterhood!

The challenges of liberation theology go a good way towards this reality. Liberation theology demands rediscovery of the bedrock commitment to justice in the meaning of 'kingdom of heaven' and the mission of the church.

> And it shall come to pass afterward, that I will pour out my spirit on all flesh; your sons and your daughters shall prophesy, your old men shall dream dreams, and your young men shall see visions. Even upon the menservants and maidservants in those days, I will pour out my spirit (Joel 2.28f.).

Liberation theology is born in poverty and despotism. When truth is sought in these terrible places of misery and helplessness, only a suffering God can help. God's way with this world is the way of the cross, of death and resurrection. Liberation theology offers this daunting truth as the gift of the poor to the rich: for in asking for a just share of the world's resources, the poor recall us to some central gospel imperatives. Our obligation as Christians is to receive the gift of the poor and to incarnate their struggles in our own economic status quo, thereby realizing that charity that does not really hurt our pockets is no more than sentimental eyewash. In this realization we are recalled to the highest counsels of Christ.

Nearer home, the environmentalists are finding pithy and unsentimental ways of cherishing our earth for those who have, as yet, no say in how we spend our riches, and for whom present Western patterns of technological excess and greed are destroying the all-too-precarious future.

> *They shall not hurt or destroy in all my holy mountain; for the earth shall be full of the knowledge of the Lord as the waters cover the sea (Isa. 11.9).*

Movements like Greenpeace and Friends of the Earth conjure fantasies of cavorting dolphins, killer whales kissing brave trainers, small boats pitting their courage against powerful whaling ships who appear ruthlessly determined to exterminate an entire species for private gain. The reality of what they are doing, however, often misses the pages of the *Mirror*. Their brief is profoundly simple. Recognizing that all matter and energy needed for life moves in closed circles from which 'nothing escapes and to which only the driving fire of the sun is added', Friends of the Earth work towards providing the best possible information, written for the thoughtful lay person, about the action needed to meet current threats to the environment. They encourage a humble respect for our planet:

> Man does not like to think his history is short, but so it is – so short that it is the merest instant in the earth's history. To see this, to put man's life in context with the earth's, imagine the whole history of the earth compressed into the six-day week of the biblical creation – a scale that makes eight thousand years pass in a single second. The first day and a half of this week are too early for life, which does not appear until about Tuesday noon. During the rest of Tuesday, and also Wednesday, Thursday, Friday, and well into Saturday, life expands and transforms the planet: life becomes more diverse, more stable, more beautiful; life makes a home for itself and adapts itself to live there.

At four in the afternoon on Saturday, the age of reptiles comes on-stage; at nine in the evening it goes off-stage, but pelicans and redwoods are already here, life forms now threatened by man's wish to have the whole world to himself. Man does not appear on the earth until three minutes before Saturday midnight. A second before midnight, man the hunter becomes man the farmer, and wandering tribesmen become villagers. Two-fifths of a second before midnight, Tutenkhamon rules Egypt. A third of a second before midnight, K'ung fu-tzu and Gautama Buddha walk the earth. A fortieth of a second before midnight, the Industrial Revolution begins. It is midnight now, and some people are saying we can go on at the rate that has worked for this fortieth of a second, because we know all the answers. Do we really know that much? ... We have forgotten how to be good guests, how to walk lightly on the earth as its other creatures do.[8]

Proponents of ecology have pointed the finger at Christianity as the originator of a debased view of nature, as a religious sanction for modern technogical exploitation. As Christian feminists we are all too aware that dominion has turned to domination, but would see this as having more to do with the break-up of communal tribal society, the subsequent founding of urban culture, and (just as importantly) literalist interpretations of early scriptures than with the phenomenon of Christianity itself. We would point to a post-technological religion of reconciliation with the earth. And in the more immediately foreseeable future, we would hope to see a covenant with the poor and wretched of the earth, human as well as animal, to emerge from the ecology movement.

> And they shall beat their swords into ploughshares, and their spears into pruning hooks; nation shall not lift up sword against nation, neither shall they learn war any more (Isa. 2.4).

No utopian or Christian new covenant can be truly workable in a world where a balance of terror is an instrument of international dealings. The most radical and far-sighted works of justice and mercy are overturned at the push of a button. To talk about the peace movement we have to talk in specifics. More and more men and women are taking what is known as the unilateralist position. Those who hold to this faith of the absurd do not simply think that peace is a good thing and will happily disarm if 'the others do'; they are not even those who fight for Amnesty and the Third

World. They are the men and women who maintain that we must take the risks of peace upon ourselves, here and now, rather than impose the risks of war upon the world. Those who take this stand are often dismissed as cranks at best and traitors at worst. But they, above all, maintain the gospel ideal of non-violence as a response to the world's hunger and to God's promise that all life is precious.

At the moment of sharing the cup at the last supper, Christ taught his disciples that God's way of suffering love was directly opposed to secular power and striving for cult survival or cult supremacy: 'The kings of the Gentiles exercise lordship over them; and those in authority over them are called benefactors. But not so with you; rather let the greatest among you become as the youngest, and the leader as one who serves' (Luke 22.24–27). It shall not be so among you. The promise that we are infinitely precious is a haunting gospel theme: 'The hairs of your head are all numbered'; 'Seek first the Kingdom of God, and all these things shall be added unto you.' Somehow our survival will be taken care of.

There is in the peace movement a rich seed-bed of Christian inspiration; but the history of the church and war, summed up in the 'just war' tradition which has dominated since the fifth century, has largely removed the gospel imperative of non-violence from its centrality. The just war tradition is only one formal system of dogma which has turned Christian teaching on its head (though few of the present and proposed wars going on in the world would fulfil its conditions). One can see in the following statement the back-to-the-wall barbarism of a power controlled church at its most extreme:

> When the existence of the church is threatened, she is released from the commandments of morality. With unity as the end, the use of every means is sanctified, even cunning, treachery, violence, simony, prison, death. For all order is for the sake of the community, and the individual must be sacrificed to the common good.[9]

The just war tradition, which can be described as the thin edge of such a terrible wedge, permits Christians to act as citizen soldiers in a way that would have been unthinkable to earlier Christians, let alone Christ himself.

The present imminent prospect of global annihilation forces us to contemplate the imbalances of human thinking that have brought us to this tragic brink. As we begin to see the connection between today's insanity and the absence of women's thoughts from the processes of culture and history-making, we dare to propose that the hidden history of women, as mothers and nurturers, has not removed them culturally from first principles. In this nuclear-fragile age women's contribution to history and theology might well be to teach the world to stay alive. Germaine Greer prophesied the present challenge to feminist insight as long ago as 1970: 'If women would only offer a genuine alternative to the treadmill of violence, the world might breathe a little longer with less pain.'[10] (Updated in preface to second edition, p. xxiii.)

The nuclear debate today is indeed a life and death debate. Modern stockpiling and the toys we terrify each other with are deadly for the whole planet. Death, if it comes (Erich Fromm cryptically observed that we have never created a weapon and then *not* used it), will be the unthinkable mega-death; the old principles for which wars were fought, and for which no doubt World War Three will be fought, will have no meaning. The historian E. P. Thompson clarifies the ethical idiocy of present policies:

> Those who have supported the policy of deterrence have done so in the confidence that this policy would prevent nuclear war from taking place.[11] They have not contemplated the alternatives and have been able to avoid facing certain questions raised by that alternative. First: is nuclear war preferable to being overcome by the enemy?
>
> Are the deaths of 15 or 20 million people and the utter destruction of the country preferable to an occupation which might offer the possibility, after some years, of resurgence and recuperation? Second: are we prepared to endorse the use of such weapons against the innocent, the children and the aged of an 'enemy'?[12]

Significantly, women are often in the majority at peace meetings and disarmament rallies. A historical and cultural depth to female experience gives them a real interest in survival, not because they are somehow more gentle or in any way less prone to absorb the scientific and political expertise that goes along with conventional wisdom about 'defence', but because 'Men must work and women must weep' is all too true in human history. The lethal and heart-rending effects of men's deadly works are too terrible to quench either tears or protest, however much either remains unheeded. The female experience of motherhood, largely unmentioned in the history of conquest and defeat, has its own stories to tell. If we are to claim that we have learnt the values needed for survival today and that our experiences must be incorporated into history-making to save the world, then it is appropriate to look at women's history in war.

We are the first generation to be raised on television views of the inescapably ugly side of war. Our screens flicker with the bodies and faces of the women and children of Vietnam, Kampuchea, Uganda, the Middle East, Northern Ireland. But for most of recorded history women's participation has appeared peripheral. The sharp images that come to mind are very often the dangerously sentimental ones of keeping the home fires burning. Brought up, as we were, on the feminine mystique of the 1950s and 1960s, children of a war in which real heroes really died to deliver the world from Hitler, our earlier technicolour images were of women waving goodbye with moist eyes and a dreamy look into the ethical middle distance. Our youth culture as well as our history lessons were full of noble sacrificial women who gave courage to the heroes, from the mothers of Sparta who told their sons to come back with their shields or on them, to the women of World War One who sent white feathers to the 'cowards' who refused to fight in that dynastic quarrel of power, privilege and patriarchy.

Women have sanctioned violence as an unquestioned reality, sometimes even welcomed it as a spurious token of regard, in such crude ways as inciting brawls or duels. They have allowed themselves to become part of the victor's laurel[13] in terms of sexual access or by being dreamed of as 'England, Home and Beauty'.

More often, female protest has been silenced by the sheer horrors of war. It was unthinkable that the millions, 'half the seed of Europe',[14] who died in World War One should have died in vain, that those who said so were called traitors. Harsh, unequivocal protest has best survived in satirical form, brilliantly poeticized in such works as *Oh What a Lovely War!* of our day and *Lysistrata* of Aristophanes, where women took the never-to-be-repeated (why?) step of refusing to sleep with their warrior lovers until the Athenians and Spartans made peace.

Women have usually broken their hearts and picked up the pieces. Women on the battlefield picking up severed limbs, clearing up the mess of their homes and lives, hated the cause but knew that if they did not heal and comfort there would be no human presence at all amid the carnage. There's the catch. Broken severed bodies and lives do not inspire rebellion or the further anarchy of mockery and protest. But the women, the mothers know that if men had suckled the young soldiers at their own breasts or brought them forth from their own bodies, they would not so lightly send them to slaughter, and they would certainly never give the slaughter such high-sounding titles as 'honour', 'a far greater thing' or the ultimate blasphemy, 'My country right or wrong'. Adrienne Rich wrote: 'Women upon whom most of the burden of respect for life is placed know that it is not an absolute value in history. We know too much at firsthand about the violence of the warrior, the rapist, the institutional violence of political and social systems in which we have little part but which affects our bodies, our children, our ageing parents – the violence which over centuries we have been told is the way of the world but which *we exist to mitigate and assuage*' (italics ours).[15]

> *For the Lord has created a new thing on the earth: a woman protects a man (Jer. 31.22).*

Feminist vision would hope that women as the bearers and not the makers of culture, in their day-to-day experiences of birth, blood and death, may have learned the kind of universality and compassion that wills nobody's death. Our history in the story of women and violence is being told now in our efforts to reclaim our bodies and our lives. Our wombs, our bodies, have been the basis on which culture has been built, as well as the raw material of cannon fodder. It is at this point of oneness with all human life, rather than as the makers of history or 'our way of life', that we can be now truly upholders of human survival in the face of nuclear insanity.

Our male-dominated church and male-supremacist society encourage a false veneration of motherhood, a mystification of the feminine that is used, politically and spiritually, as a weapon against female demand to be included in the formal processes of history. 'But you can have babies', is a frequently reiterated comeback to female energy and ambition.[16]

The church has at times in its history upheld the sanctity of human fertility and sexuality; but these assertions have been so fraught with ambiguity and mystique that in fact Christian thinking has combined with secular exploitation of the vulnerability of women and children. (The church, not the state, named children 'illegitimate'.) A revered thinker like C. S. Lewis used the powerful emotional tie of mothers and children as an argument for male leadership. If the family and wider societal groups have to have headship, he said, then that head must be a man. What woman, said Lewis, would give a second thought to civilized ideals of justice and fairness where the health and happiness of her own children were at stake? Women are thus given the 'mother tiger' role of defence and total physical care of the young – while man imbues, from a remote distance, the higher ideals of culture. Freudian analysis is about making this happen – helping the boy escape the till-now venerated sphere and join 'real life'. If woman accepts this role, total responsibility then unfits her for any other role than she-animal (though there are indications that mother tigers have a higher than human code). The noble savage is romanticized, then colonized and controlled.

We can see an urging of the traditional role as sacred in the backlash writings of today; we can also see the respect that we can expect to receive if we fulfil the role. Arianna Stassinopolous, in her counterblast to feminist thinking,[17] wrote: 'Bearing and giving birth to a child is an experience not comparable with any other. At no other time is a human being so near to creation, so near to affirming life and glimpsing immortality.' Then, after blaming feminists who resist this definition by anatomy, she says: 'Do women really see motherhood in this way? Or does it provide a role which largely releases them from the existential anxieties of today; from the pervasive problem of meaninglessness, that increasingly overrides the problem of frustration? What am I here for? What is it that I want out of life? How can I use my freedom? The woman has an answer in her baby.' In another part of her book, with the aim of showing how women should keep out of armies (a very glaring example of her many 'Aunt Sallies' – feminist demand for participation in the armed forces is minimal, for reasons that this chapter hopes to show), Stassinopolous demonstrates just how much respect motherhood will be and has been accorded by those who are allowed to make history: 'There are strong demographic reasons why a nation dare not put its women in an army. If a society loses a large number of men in a war it can, if it wishes, make up the population losses in one generation by legalizing polygamy or by encouraging illegitimate breeding.'[18] As monogamous mothers, whose sacred function in this 'wicked world' of women's libbers is upheld by Father Church and Mother Arianna, this statement does not exactly fill us with confidence!

The simple truth is that female fertility has always been politicized, mystified, privatized, legislated over and ultimately shortchanged. Some of the most oppressive regimes in the history of the world have venerated motherhood – Augustus Caesar; the 'Kinder,

Kirche, Küche' of Nazi ideology; the angel-in-the-house image of Victorian wives, whose darker shadows in the coal mines of the Midlands, cotton mills of Lancashire and the train to Dachau show the true violence of the institution when its value depends on the megalomaniacal dreams of those who would worship us. A powerful amplification of this point is made in Alice Meynell's poem 'Parentage':

> *When Augustus Caesar legislated against the unmarried citizens of Rome, he declared them to be, in some sort, slayers of the people*
>
> Ah no, not these!
> These who were childless, are not they who gave
> So many dead unto the journeying wave,
> The helpless nurselings of the cradling seas;
> Not they who, doomed by infallible decrees
> unnumbered man to the innumerable grave. –
> But those who slay are fathers. Theirs are armies. Death is theirs –
> The death of innocences and despairs;
> The dying of the golden and the grey.
> The sentence, when these speak it, has no Nay.
> And she who slays is she who bears, who bears.[19]

Exploitation of female fertility by the 'higher' powers of civilization is ignominious indeed, and is documented by such feminist writers as Mary Daly in *Gyn/Ecology*, Adrienne Rich in *Of Woman Born*, and in the feminist theology of Rosemary Radford Ruether and Mary Condren. In our own time, we have seen how 'enlightened' provisions for abortion or contraception have been made available or withdrawn from women according to political and demographic needs in society.[20]

It is no wonder that the need to reclaim our own bodies is seen as a primary aim of feminism. Small wonder, too, that some feminists have judged it a black day for women when men discovered that it was their seed, not the earth or wind or the gods, that made new life grow inside a woman's body! Stassinopolous claims: 'Liberation is the denial of any intrinsic value to maternity.'[21] How wrong she is.

The theme of motherhood is providing a rich body of poetic thought and literature from feminist writers and scholars. This literature explores both the destructiveness of our present practices and the positive potential of human parenthood; at its most prophetic, it contains exciting possibilities for Christians to peel away the layers of patriarchy that have covered and petrified its traditions, and to recall the Christian community to a four-square commitment to non-violence and justice.

Earlier in the book we outlined some of the ways in which society has nostalgically projected on to the church the near-invisible virtues of nurture, tenderness, caring. The church has in turn (perhaps for fear of being too tenderly thought of and discarded as unreal) mystified and twisted the tough first principles of the gospel into the tamely domesticated virtues of 'Christian marriage and family life'. This process, in the given realities of our society, inevitably apportions the earthly physical tasks involved in loving young children, in tending and cherishing homes and the immediate environment, to half the human race. Feminist prophecy would see this dangerous division having profound effects not only on the lives of women but in the wider environment of the earth itself – of the whole human family. Christian pacifists claim that by allowing Christ's first commandment of love to be imprisoned in clan and family chauvinism, we ignore his promises, break his body anew, and bring about the extinction of God's creation. The language of death and resurrection is real enough in the challenges of the peace message of Jesus, and it is this language that is being spoken today by those feminists who claim that only the 'death' of motherhood as an institution will end the age-old conspiracy of men and women to keep history in the thrall of death-merchants.

What is astonishing, what can give us enormous hope and belief in a future in which the lives of women and children shall be mended and rewoven by women's hands, is all that we have managed to salvage, of ourselves, for our children, even within the destructiveness of the institution: the tenderness, the passion, the trust in our instincts, the evocation of a courage we did not know we owned, the detailed apprehension of another human existence, the full realization of the cost and precariousness of life. The mother's battle for her child – with sickness, with poverty, with war, with all the forces of exploitation and callousness which cheapen human life – needs to become a common human battle, waged in love and in the passion for survival. But for this to happen, the institution (not the *fact*) of motherhood must be destroyed. The changes required to make this possible reverberate into every part of the patriarchal system.

To destroy the institution is not to abolish motherhood. It is to release the creation and sustenance of life into the same realm of decision, struggle, surprise, imagination and conscious intelligence, as any other difficult, but freely chosen work.[22]

Yes! The more life-affirming experiences of women must not be romanticized but politicized. Gandhi pointed out that family life is about the working out of the possibilities of love in day-to-day conflicts. 'Little quarrels of millions of families in their daily lives disappear before the exercise of this force (Gandhi speaks here of *Satyagraha*, or love-force). History is really a record of every interruption of the even working of love in the reconciliation of differences, and what is true of families and communities is true of nations.'[23] Perhaps that's a rather romantic view of what goes on at 47, Acacia Drive; but it is more and more likely to come true now that feminist consciousness is making deep inroads into private structures of injustice. The anger, helplessness and loneliness felt by an exiled suburban housewife, or by any mother removed as she so often is from a supportive, warm and varied community, is a vital part of feminist articulation of the theme of motherhood. Unfortunately, this kind of anger is the only side of the predicament to be picked up by the media or noted by opponents, and is thus seen as threatening.[24]

Many Christians and opponents of feminism fear the language of confrontation being brought into the hallowed sanctuary of the home. There is indeed a great deal of feminist polemic which lays bare the anger that women have always known as guardians of new life; that they speak from a position of weakness, having to operate within the double bind of having little say in the way in which the community is run while taking responsibility for all its human values. But anger and impatience are only part of the story, and we must emphasize an important part of the healing too. The breadth of feminist demand includes a new deal not just from men but for men. Behind all the 'woman's page' chat about Dad changing nappies and letting Super-mum do a job (so easily dismissible as cosy middle-class chic) is a real demand that the values and 'authenticity' of child-rearing must be experienced by men, too, in order to be effectively incorporated into our public culture and ethical system. This process is one of restoration – of restoring men to their tears and their children, on the premise that vaunting the values of motherhood and home as a private haven of bliss, as the only thing that makes sense in this wicked world, is at least as

dangerous as saying that mothering is a trivial and unmanly occupation. Mothering, as St Francis pointed out long ago, is like
charity itself – it may well begin at home but when it stays at home
it ceases to be either.

In her book *The Rocking of the Cradle and the Ruling of the
World*, Professor Dorothy Dinnerstein details the many ways that
men and women conspire to separate the concerns of private and
public life. Men are often insensitive to the seriousness of the lethal
projects they initiate because they are brought up to see themselves
removed from the vulnerability of human babies. If we were to
change radically the ways we care for the young and weak, the
lives of both sexes could be restored to full potential and we could
begin to turn history from its present destructive path. How can
men be arbiters of justice or makers of peace while they remain so
remote from the helplessness of the weak and the cycles of nature?
Dinnerstein extends her audacious thesis by asserting: 'When males
are as directly involved as females in the intensely carnal lives of
infants and small children, the reality of the male body as a source
of new creatures is bound to become substantial for us at an earlier
age than it does now.'[25] This new reality will remain a stronger
emotional and spiritual reality afterwards. This would free women
to be seen as equally capable of what we now think of as the higher
business of civilization, together with men, who sharing their point
of view will not consign women's insights to 'the feminine point
of view'.

Dinnerstein is an academic psychologist. She has absorbed the
breadth of Freudian understanding without succumbing to its fatalism. She does not see the roles of the sexes as biologically
determined. She does not see women as innately more concerned
with the body than men are. Her book proposes that cultural sex
role differentiation is a direct result of our practice of putting
women in exclusive control of small babies. Her conclusion is that
the only way we can create strong and loving people for a just
world is to share the nurture of that world's citizens. Our conventional sociological wisdom and present normative opinions (for
example, 'but women can go back to work when the children are
old enough', 'lots of men help out at home . . . ', 'you shouldn't
have children if you don't want to look after them . . .', 'there's
plenty of time later to change the world. . .') are re-examined and
overturned by Dinnerstein's vision. While we might have reserva-
tions about the extreme terms in which the consequences of
single-sex child-rearing are presented in her gigantic and complex

book, the realization that feminist thought is imagining a real and concrete programme for survival makes now a most exciting time to be alive.

There is something magical and liberating to the human spirit when we can read in the life-work and wise words of another – a woman we have never met – a conceptualizing of our unease with the wisdom of teachers and fathers. This experience can articulate a previously stammering rage. We can say, 'Yes, that's it! That was what I was trying to say!'; we can turn present loss of words into an ungrudging 'I wish I'd said that!' Dorothy Dinnerstein is not a Christian; neither is Adrienne Rich, the poet whose words begin and permeate this chapter. But implicit in all their sometimes difficult language is a call to experience the resurrection of our most cherished institutions to their full potential. A vision of resurrection is what we, the church, and the world need to carry us through the wounds of today. The pilgrimage undertaken by brave and far-seeing sisters has already shown so much love and possibility. How strong we feel in our exploration alongside our secular sisters, and how awed in our present task of bringing some of this strength to the church. There can be no turning back.

So much of the celebration of the female body and its power to create life – now coming out of feminist thinking – comes from the strength given by the women who went before. Many, like Simone de Beauvoir, denied their own fertility to begin to imagine a world where women would not be defined by their biology. These are the giants of women's history on whose shoulders we stand. That we are able to trust our bodies, our motherhood, is a tribute to their testimonies and sacrifice. That we can now make the journey back to our bodies with joy is a tribute to how far the movement has sustained and supported us. All female achievement has been 'in spite of' – in spite of four children, ten children, the sorrows of childlessness, wifehood – in spite of singleness, attributed as often as not to some kind of sexual pathology or another. This observation will possibly bring the more mindless of our critics to say, 'Ah! they are beginning to realize their true function and come at last to home truths, I knew all this ephemeral Women's Lib. wouldn't last.' Will the deepest parts of our psyche – where we are most vulnerable, gentle and generous, be wide open to the rapist again? We think not. We end up where we started, and see our bodies and ourselves as if for the first time.

The church contains an irreplaceable gospel, and the organization, for all its weakness and betrayal of that gospel, has shed the light of God's saints upon the world. Belief in the implications of our membership of this fellowship of believers, which so honours and reveres motherhood in its highest symbolism, and yet fails in its daily life to give place to female wisdom, nonetheless gives us strength to speak our truth. Paradoxically, it is in our traditional roles as wives and mothers that our political and spiritual radicalism is most profoundly experienced.

The vision that sustains us is worth staking our lives on. We are not alone; we are telling our stories to each other, and we are insistently sharing the stories and the vision with the church. The church has always had a hard time believing that the first could be last and the meek inherit the earth. We know in our souls that such knowledge is the beginning of Wisdom, personified in the Old Testament as a woman, wild and unladylike, shouting aloud in the streets for bread and justice because no one in the synagogue, or the courts, or the laws of the land would listen. Her Greek sister Cassandra, whose story introduced the first chapter of this book, has grown up a good deal, too. Cassandra's Christian counterpart still loves Apollo. Apollo's heat and light are still splendidly dazzling to her; but he's a bit puzzled that Cassandra, formerly such a good girl, no longer silently acquiesces to his definition of her. No longer are seduction, sycophancy and idolatrous slavery the order of the day. Once Apollo (read patriarchal religion) gets past this particular identity crisis, he and Cassandra can together rebuild the temple and the world. Until then, this book and this story are not ending.

> Breathe on the embers of our failing hearts
> O God;
> Kindle in us a hunger
> For wholeness and goodness,
> For the dawning of a new world.
>   Amen.

Notes

Chapter 1 Daughters of the Enlightenment

1. We limit our list of recommended reading to three publications available in this country: Jacob Needleman and George Baker (eds.), *Understanding the New Religions*, Seabury Press, New York 1978; Rosemary Radford Ruether and Eleanor McLaughlin, *Women of Spirit*, Simon & Schuster, New York 1979; Rosemary Radford Ruether, *Women and Religion in America: The Nineteenth Century*, Vol. I, Harper & Row, New York 1981.

2. Mary Evans and David Morgan, *Work on Women: A Guide to the Literature*, Tavistock Publications 1979.

3. Quoted in Julia O'Faolain and Lauro Martinez (eds.), *Not in God's Image*, Virago 1979, p. 317.

4. Quoted in Claire Tomalin, *The Life and Death of Mary Wollstonecraft*, Penguin Books 1977, pp. 36f.

5. Mary Wollstonecraft, *A Vindication of the Rights of Women* (1792), edited by Miriam Brody Kramnick, Penguin Books 1975, p. 85.

6. Tomalin, op. cit., p. 293.

7. Ibid.

8. John Stuart Mill, *The Subjection of Women* (1869). Excerpts can be found in Alice Rossi, *The Feminist Papers: From Adams to de Beauvoir*, Bantam Books, New York 1974, pp. 196–238.

9. George Eliot, *Middlemarch* (1871), Penguin Books, p. 896.

10. Joan and Kenneth Macksey, *The Guinness Guide to Feminine Achievements*, Guinness Superlatives 1975, p. 83.

11. Midge Mackenzie, *Shoulder to Shoulder*, Penguin 1975, p. 320.

12. Quoted in Marie Fortune and Joann Haugerud (eds.), *Study Guide to the Woman's Bible*, Coalition Task Force on Women and Religion, Seattle 1975, p. 11.

13. Temperance movements flourished in the nineteenth century. Hatchet-wielding Kansas-born Carrie A. Nation is probably the best known among the women on the 'lunatic fringes'.

14. These women are household names. A good record of their activities is Leslie B. Tanner (ed.), *Voices from Women's Liberation*, Mentor 1970.

15. The Church of England social welfare agency – now named Welcare – which works largely with single mothers.

16. *Feminist Theology and Women Priests. An Introduction and Annotated Bibliography*, SCM Publications 1977, p. 23.

17. An excellent account of Catherine Booth's life and character can be found in Ray Strachey, *The Cause: A Short History of the Women's Movement in Great Britain*, Virago 1978, pp. 213ff.

18. Feminist resurgence in the last ten years or so has led to popular interest in the history of the suffragettes. Midge Mackenzie (*Shoulder to Shoulder*) was one of the originators of a popular BBC dramatized television series of the same title. One does not have to go far though to encounter old chestnuts like: 'It was the good work women did in the Great War that got them the vote, not the extravagant behaviour of the few trouble-makers', implying that activism is counter-productive and women will only get 'rewarded' rights for good behaviour. However unfortunately true this may sometimes be, such a smug attitude does not take into account the vision and courage of the women involved in the suffrage campaign or the treachery of many contemporary politicians.

19. Emma Goldman's life and work are recounted in Emma Goldman, *The Traffic in Women and Other Essays on Feminism*, Times Change Press, New York 1970.

20. Virginia Woolf, *Three Guineas*, The Hogarth Press 1938; Penguin Books 1977 (the quotation is from pp. 72f. of the Penguin edition).

21. Theodore Roszak, 'The Hard and the Soft', in *Masculine/Feminine: Readings in Sexual Mythology and the Liberation of Women*, ed. by Betty and Theodore Roszak, Harper & Row, New York 1969, pp. 87–104.

22. Ibid., p. 93.

23. In J. Beecher and R. Bienvenu (eds.), *The Utopian Vision of Charles Fourier: Selected Writings*, Beacon Press, Boston 1971, pp. 195f.

24. Simone de Beauvoir, *The Second Sex*, Cape 1968; Penguin Books 1972.

25. Roszak, op. cit., p. 103.

26. Rossi, op. cit., pp. 672–4.

27. When questioned about unemployment figures in the England of the 1980s, a Tory MP said that the numbers could not be compared with the 1930s because many of today's unemployed are women!

28. Betty Friedan, *The Feminine Mystique*, Penguin Books 1965, pp. 13–30.

29. Ibid., p. 305.

30. Betty Friedan, *It Changed My Life*, Gollancz 1977, pp. 157–69.

31. John A. T. Robinson, *Honest to God*, SCM Press 1963.

32. The widespread public debate following the publication of Robinson's book was unprecedented for a work of theology in our century. A subsequent publication, David L. Edwards and John A. T. Robinson (eds.), *The Honest to God Debate*, SCM Press 1963, summarizes public reaction. Although revolutionary theology by no means came to a standstill after the mid 1960s (witness Hans Küng et al.), no other work has stirred such secular interest.

33. It is by now commonplace to point out that much of the impetus for the present movement came from young idealistic women relegated to

tea and typing in the many radical movements of the 1960s. Stokely Carmichael's unequivocal put-down has passed into feminist folklore: 'The only place for women in the SNCC is prone', quoted in Germaine Greer, *The Female Eunuch*, Paladin 1971, p. 301.

Chapter 2 Daughters of Eve

1. Students of the Bible will note direct parallels with the story of Lot and Sodom in Genesis 19. However, the guests in the Sodom story have miraculous powers and strike the wicked Sodomites with blindness (Gen. 19.11).

2. F. Davidson, A. M. Stibbs and E. F. Kevan (eds.), *The New Bible Commentary*, Inter-Varsity Fellowship 1953, p. 256.

3. H. H. Rowley (ed.), *Peake's Commentary on the Bible*, Nelson 1962, p. 314.

4. Charles M. Lawson (ed.), *The Interpreter's One Volume Commentary on the Bible*, Abingdon Press, Nashville 1971 and Collins 1972, p. 149.

5. Elizabeth Cady Stanton, *The Woman's Bible*, republished by Coalition Task Force on Women and Religion, Seattle 1974, Part II, p. 16.

6. Quoted in Marie Fortune and Joann Haugerud (eds.), *Study Guide to the Woman's Bible*, Coalition Task Force on Women and Religion, Seattle 1975, p. 3.

7. The Talmud is the collection of Jewish commentary on scripture and oral tradition, compiled formally during the early centuries of Christianity. It is divided into six parts: Seeds, Feasts, Women and Marriage, Civil and Criminal Law, Sacrifices, Clean and Unclean Things and their Purification.

8. In spite of her impressive scholarship, Miss Smith was never invited to participate in the many contemporary projects of biblical translation and revision.

9. For further details of activities in this period see Rosemary Radford Ruether, *Women and Religion in America: The Nineteenth Century*, Vol. 1, Harper and Row, New York 1981.

10. There is an excellent summary of male legal rights under patriarchy in Phyllis Bird, 'Images of Women in the Old Testament', in *Religion and Sexism*, edited by Rosemary Radford Ruether, Simon and Schuster, New York 1974, pp. 41–88.

11. Among these educated women, note Priscilla (Acts 18.26); Phoebe the deacon (Rom. 16.1); Euodia and Syntyche (Phil. 4.2) and the office of widow (I Tim. 5.3ff.).

12. There follows a discussion of covering the head: 'For man was not made from woman, but woman from man. Neither was man created for woman, but woman for man. That is why a woman ought to have a veil on her head, because of the angels.' Angels were thought to administer the divine order. Bare-headed or shorn women worshipping in the presence of men showed disrespect for this order.

13. Gnosticism came into prominence in the second century. 'Gnosis' is Greek for 'knowledge' – a special knowledge of the divine mysteries which was reserved for an elect group of 'knowers'. The Gnosticism of

the second-century sects 'can be summed up in the idea of a divine spark in man, deriving from the divine realm, fallen into this world of fate, birth and death, and needing to be awakened by the divine counterpart of the self in order to be finally reintegrated' (R. McL. Wilson, *Gnosis and the New Testament*, Blackwell 1968, p. 17, quoting from papers discussed at the Messina Colloquium 1966). More recent studies continue to shed light on the problems of the origins of Gnosticism (see n. 15).

14. E. Hennecke (ed.), *New Testament Apocrypha*, Vol. 1, SCM Press ²1973, p. 522.

15. Elaine Pagels, *The Gnostic Gospels*, Weidenfeld and Nicolson 1979. This last concept was incorporated later into mediaeval monasticism as 'virginal feminism' (see Ruether, *Religion and Sexism*, pp. 150–83), so the concept of self was still male-centred but women were permitted, it seems, a theology of equality.

16. Quoted by Constance Parvey, 'The Theology and Leadership of Women in the New Testament,' in Ruether, *Religion and Sexism*, p. 126.

17. *The Oxford Annotated Bible*, Oxford University Press, New York 1962, p. 1408.

18. Krister Stendahl, *The Bible and the Role of Women*, Fortress Press, Philadelphia 1966, p. 33.

19. Stendahl, ibid.

Chapter 3 Daughters and Lovers

1. I.e., the fear that there would be widespread abandoning of middle-aged wives and a form of (male-controlled) serial polygamy.

2. Monica Furlong, *With Love to the Church*, Hodder and Stoughton 1965, ch. 3.

3. John Newsome defending his report in *The Observer*, 11 October 1964. Quoted by Eva Figes, *Patriarchal Attitudes*, Faber 1970, p. 30.

4. Erica Jong, *Fear of Flying*, Holt, Rinehart and Winston, New York 1973, and Secker and Warburg 1974.

5. Betty Friedan, *The Feminine Mystique*, Penguin Books 1965.

6. Adrienne Rich, *Of Woman Born*, Norton, New York 1976, and Virago 1977, p. 57.

7. Part of the consciousness of this group is to rejoice in the labels they attract. 'I am a monster,' says Robin Morgan in her poem of that name, 'and I am Proud.' Mary Daly's *Gyn/Ecology*, Beacon Press, Boston 1978, contains probably the most comprehensive list of this phenomenon. She explores the many terms of abuse levelled throughout history at women – 'hag', 'crone', 'witch', 'spinster', and transforms them into hymns of strength and autonomy.

8. *Spare Rib*, 27 Clerkenwell Close, London EC1, Issue 93, April 1980, p. 38.

9. Rosemary Radford Ruether and Eleanor McLaughlin (eds.), *Women of Spirit*, Simon and Schuster, New York 1979, p. 19.

10. See especially two pamphlets: Harry Williams, *The Gay Christian Movement and the Education of Public Opinion*, Gay Christian Move-

ment, Box 6914, London WC1, 1979, and Jim Cotter (ed.), *Exploring Lifestyles*, GCM 1980. The more widely publicized responses are Anglican, Methodist and Roman Catholic: Peter Coleman, *Christian Attitudes to Homosexuality*, SPCK 1980; General Synod Board of Social Responsibility, *Homosexual Relationships*, CIO Publishing 1979; A. Kosnick et al., *Human Sexuality*, Search Press 1977; Una Kroll, *Sexual Counselling*, SPCK 1980; John J. McNeill SJ, *The Church and the Homosexual*, Darton, Longman and Todd 1977; Methodist Board of Social Responsibility, *A Christian Understanding of Human Sexuality*, 1980; Basil and Rachel Moss, *Humanity and Sexuality*, CIO Publishing 1978.

11. Adrienne Rich comments: 'Vulgar psychoanalytic opinion has it that "the son of the mother" becomes homosexual either in flight from the power of women, or in protest against the traditional male role. In reality we know next to nothing about the influences and accidents which lead to erotic love for one's own sex. Why men choose men instead of women for sexual gratification, or as life partners, is a question which cannot be answered simplistically in terms of fifth century Athens; nor in terms of the "effeminizing" of sons by mothers who want to "hold on to them" ' (*Of Women Born*, pp. 209f.).

12. Private correspondence.

13. Jim Cotter in *Christian Action Journal*, Autumn 1979, pp. 18–20.

14. New 'certain' methods of creating fewer and more wanted children are almost exclusively biologically centred in the female body. Feminist critique of the Pill and the IUD is threefold: (*a*) they are physically dangerous and sometimes lethal; (*b*) they are a failure in the midst of so much more safe and advanced life-preserving achievement, and unlikely to be so unsatisfactory were men's bodies affected; (*c*) they allow men to be removed from the moral arena of fertility.

15. See SCM *Movement* pamphlet no. 37, *Abortion: The Tragic Dilemma*.

16. *The World of Gwendolyn Brooks*, Harper and Row, New York 1971. © 1945 by Gwendolyn Brooks.

17. John Taylor, Bishop of Winchester, presented this prayer to be said on the termination of a pregnancy as a proposed entry in the 1980 *Alternative Service Book*: 'Heavenly Father, you are the giver of life and you share with us the care of the life that is given. Into your hands we commit in trust the developing life that we have cut short. Look in merciful judgment on the decision that we have made, and assure us in all our uncertainty that your love for us can never change.' The prayer was presented to the General Synod in November 1978 and rejected. (Our thanks to David Jarrett of Church House for details.)

18. In her book *The Dialectic of Sex*, Bantam 1971, Shulamith Firestone speaks of childbearing as a barbaric and brutalizing experience, unredeemable in or out of a patriarchal context. The alternatives she suggests are high financial incentives and rewards for breeding while we await the necessary technology leading to test-tube babies. There is increasing demand by mothers in the US to know the sex of their unborn babies and demanding abortion if this information is withheld or the sex is the 'wrong'

one, thus exploiting a liberal law to reinforce dynastic and selective breeding. At the moment choices are usually made on sexist principles of primogeniture.

Chapter 4 Sisters of the Spirit

1. Nor does this situation appear to be changing. We refer the reader to the recent book by Eric Mascall, *Whatever happened to the Human Mind?*, SPCK 1980, particularly Chapter 5, 'Sexuality and God'. In Mascall, particularly, we see the theology of subordination justifying the male-dominated social order: '... I would quote words that I have written elsewhere, in which I have emphasized the essential diversity of the two sexes and, in consequence, of the parts which each has played in the central mystery of the incarnation: "It was male human *nature* that the Son of God united to his divine person; it was a female human *person* who was chosen as his mother" ' (p.140). See also Peter Moore (ed.), *Man, Woman and Priesthood*, SPCK 1978, pp. 21ff. In this country there are numerous 'anti' pamphlets put out by the Church Literature Association, dealing with the question of priesthood. Significant similarities are that these writers appear to be addressing a limited, like-minded readership, debating Bible passages, patristics, tradition and the popular and ever-evasive issue of unity (with Rome and the Orthodox). Nowhere is there a response to the many women who are now working on traditional assumptions.

2. The following recent publications are recommended: Carol P. Christ and Judith Plaskow (eds.), *Womanspirit Rising*, Harper and Row, New York 1979; Virginia Ramey Mollenkott, *Women, Men and the Bible*, Abingdon Press, Nashville 1977 (this book is available as a study kit with three sixty-minute cassettes, the book itself and a guide book with discussion questions; its orientation is evangelical); Rosemary Radford Ruether and Eleanor McLaughlin, *Women of Spirit* (see ch. 1, note 1); Letty M. Russell, *Human Liberation in a Feminist Perspective*, Westminster Press, Philadelphia 1974.

3. Rosemary Radford Ruether, *New Woman, New Earth: Sexist Ideologies and Human Liberation*, Seabury Press, New York 1975, p. xii.

4. C. S. Lewis, 'Priestesses in the Church?', in *God in the Dock. Essays on Theology*, ed. Walter Hooper, Fount Books 1979, p. 90.

5. Private correspondence.

6. Eric Mascall, *Women Priests?*, Church Literature Association 1972, p. 15.

7. Ruether, op. cit., p. xii.

8. Private correspondence.

9. Julian of Norwich, *Revelations of Divine Love*, Penguin Books 1966, p. 68.

10. Mary Daly, *Gyn/Ecology: The Metaethics of Radical Feminism*, Beacon Press, Boston 1978, esp. 'The Second Passage', pp. 107–312.

11. Naomi Goldenberg, *The Changing of the Gods*, Beacon Press, Boston 1979, p. 15.

12. Ibid., pp. 13f.

13. Cecilia M. Ady, *The Role of Women in the Church*, CIO 1948. Information found in *Feminist Theology and Women Priests: An Introduction and Annotated Bibliography*, SCM Publications 1977.

14. We recommend particularly *Are Women Human?*, a study pack published by SCM Woman's Project (1977); *The Banished Children of Eve: An Introduction to Feminist Theology*, SCM *Movement* pamphlet; *Why Men Priests? The Effects of Male Domination in the Church*, SCM Publications 1978. The first two are currently unavailable: demands for resurrection should be addressed to SCM Publications, now at PO Box 532, 40 Moat Lane, Birmingham B55 BE. Also recommended is *Churchwomanship in a Man's World. A Supplement to Christian Action Journal* 2, Spring 1978. The quarterly *Women Speaking*, published and edited by Dr Esther Hodge, 70 Westmount Road, London SE9 1LE, is a unifying periodical for women's activities and problems. This quarterly unfailingly gives space to the specific problems of women within traditional religious institutions. The Christian Women's Information and Resource Service (CWIRS), c/o Mary Pepper, Blackfriars, Oxford, provides a list of service groups, as well as gathering information on projects and communities. At present, the most comprehensive bibliography in feminist theology is by Clare B. Fischer, *Breaking Through*, Berkeley: Center for Women and Religion and the Graduate Theological Union Library 1980.

15. Groups such as the Christian Parity Group have spent a good deal of their resources and energy on arranging visits of American women priests to this country. In some cases the visits have been to encourage and share experiences with UK supporters, in some the women priests have felt it right and necessary to celebrate communion with their friends here.

16. John A. T. Robinson, *The New Reformation?*, SCM Press 1965, p. 75.

17. Particularly helpful is Sheila Collins, *A Different Heaven and Earth*, The Addison Press, Valley Forge 1974, in which she describes the main characteristics of 'herstory'. Works of fiction and poetry emphasizing women's stories as spiritual quest are discussed in Carol P. Christ, *Diving Deep and Surfacing*, Beacon Press, Boston 1980. This book reviews spiritual dimensions in the writings of Kate Chopin, Margaret Atwood, Doris Lessing, Ntozake Shange, Adrienne Rich.

18. Private correspondence.

19. Mary Welch uses the image 'From the Church Porch' as a title for her essay in the collection *Living the Faith*, edited by Kathleen Jones, Oxford University Press 1980, pp. 68–77.

20. From an unpublished statement made by Dr Pamela Tudor-Craig in response to the question, 'Why do you remain in the church?'

21. *Theology*, Vol. LXXXII, September 1979, p. 689.

22. Review of *Beyond the Fragments*, in *The Guardian*, 29 January 1980.

23. *Lilith* is an independent Jewish women's magazine, published at 250 West 57 Street, New York 10019. We refer the reader to two excellent essays in *Womanspirit Rising*, those by Judith Plaskow (pp. 179–84) and

by Aviva Cantor (pp. 185–92), and also to Judith Hauptman's essay in *Religion and Sexism*, pp. 184–212.

24. A woman priest, Jeanette Pickard, presiding over worship at St Botolph's, Aldgate, London, spoke of 'God the Creator, God the Redeemer, God the Sustainer', in place of the all-male traditional Trinity. Another suggestion for renaming God to include women's experience would be to refer to the Deity as verb ('I am', 'be-ing'), rather than noun (God the Father).

25. Eric Mascall, *Women Priests?*, pp. 23f. Early in his tract Mascall clearly states that deliberations outside the Catholic/Anglican tradition are of no real relevance to a discussion of priesthood in an apostolic context. He rather disarmingly admits to using Von Allmen's statement because it supports his own opposition to women priests!

26. A popular example of this phenomenon appears in John Updike's novel *Couples*, Penguin Books 1970. 'He thinks we've made a church of each other', says Angela of Freddy Thorne, articulating the (thwarted) hopes of close-knit, middle-class men and women striving for love and liberation without the neuroses of traditional religious dogma and practice.

27. The 'rejected' man was Professor Keith Bridstone, of the Pacific School of Religion; the story was sent to us by Mary Atwood at the School, culled from an unpublished lecture there by Susan Briehl and Deborah Steed.

Chapter 5 Daughters of the Promise

1. One of our correspondents, Yvonne Craig, is a social anthropologist, studying the effects of female ordination in the Methodist Church. Her researches will be published to coincide with the tenth anniversary of mixed ministry in 1984.

2. An opinion poll conducted by Marplan for *Now Magazine* in the spring of 1978 reveals that public approval for women's ordination is widespread: Clergy, 56% in favour and 39% opposed (5% 'don't know'); Laity, 85% in favour, 12% opposed (3% don't know). Synod voted: Bishops, 32 in favour and 17 opposed (65%/35%); Clergy, 94 in favour and 149 opposed (39%/61%); Laity, 120 in favour, 106 opposed (53%/47%). In a press conference held shortly after the synod vote, Graham Leonard, Bishop of Truro and a well-known opponent, expressed his relief that the priests in synod had shown such great theological vision. 'It is the job of the clergy to be theologically trained and to be able to point to the theological issues involved – not narrow ecclesiastical reasons but the fact that there is a relation between theology and human existence.' His opinion of the theological vision of his colleagues in the House of Bishops can easily be deduced.

3. Clifford Longley, 'Bridgehead: Women's Ordination', *The Tablet*, Vol. 232, 18 November 1978, p. 1110.

4. *Pacem in Terris*, 1963.

5. Passed in 1975 with the church safely off the hook.

6. It was reported in *The Times* during the build-up to the 1978 Synod

that a group of clergymen were preparing a demand for financial compensation should the impending pollution to the church in the persons of would-be women priests make it impossible for these men to continue in orders. This threat, however bizarre, probably did provide ballast for the schism argument.

7. 'Our vicar', writes a correspondent, 'only ever mentions women in the context of the traditional wife/mother role, although the congregation is full of women with interesting careers and achievements.'

8. Private letter.

9. The letters page of *The Times*, 11 November 1978, Fr Christopher Colven (see also n. 2 above).

10. We are told, seriously, that Rome and Constantinople look to the Church of England as the mother church and that the misdeeds of other provinces (US, Canada, New Zealand, Hong Kong) will not seriously affect unity. Indeed, when the combined strengths of these ancient communions are revived by formal unity they will be able to bring pressure to bear on the 'rebel colonies'. Can such assertions be serious? Can a priest be de-ordained? There is the precedent that women ordained in the Free Churches were required to lay aside their orders, and voluntarily did so when the Church of South India was set up in 1947.

11. As at the Lambeth Conference, July 1978.

12. Diana Collins, 'The Rehabilitation of Eve', in *Churchwomanship in a Man's World*. A Supplement to *Christian Action Journal* 2, pp. 4f.

13. Francis George Belton, *A Manual for Confessors*, Mowbray 1936.

14. Ibid., p. 109.

15. Ibid., p. 182.

16. Ibid., p. 179 (Fr Belton is quoting a friend's advice).

17. Private correspondence.

18. Ronald Millar, *Abelard and Heloise*, Act II scene 3, Samuel French 1970.

19. George Moore, *Heloise and Abelard*, Heinemann 1952, p. 408.

20. John A. T. Robinson, *The New Reformation?*, SCM Press 1965, p. 58.

21. Ibid., pp. 58f.

22. E. R. Norman is Dean of Peterhouse, Cambridge. He delivered the Reith Lectures in 1978.

23. Mary Condren, Editorial in the Supplement to *Christian Action Journal* (see n. 12 above), p. 8.

24. Attributed to Matthew Arnold.

25. Rosemary Radford Ruether, *Mary. The Feminine Face of the Church*, Westminster Press, Philadelphia 1977, p. 85; SCM Press 1979, p. 72.

26. *The Guardian*, January 1980.

27. The admission of women to this function was a matter of lengthy debate in the University Church of Christ the King in 1973. On this occasion a traditionalist head server was persuaded not to leave his post but to remain and train us properly. Because he did so, male suspicion of our motives was alleviated.

28. 'The Idea of the Mothers Union', a historical survey published in *New Dimensions*.

29. The title of Ibsen's prophetic play.

30. Private correspondence.

31. Private correspondence.

32. On 28 June 1980 a group of eight men and women staged a silent protest against yet another all-male ordination. Our leader, Monica Furlong, wrote an account of our motives and action in *The Times*, 3 July 1980, entitled, 'And the Bishops passed by on the other side'.

33. We have personally and prayerfully decided to take part in liturgical acts of disobedience. We have found ourselves much sustained by eucharists celebrated by women priests over the last few years.

34. Rosemary Radford Ruether, *New Woman, New Earth*, Seabury Press, New York 1975, p. 80.

Chapter 6 Daughters of the Reformation

1. The formidable front bench of the Movement for the Ordination of Women (Napier Hall, Hide Place, Vincent Street, London WC1) contains a committed constituency of clergy wives, as do the more activist Christian Parity Group (46 Rosehill Avenue, Sutton, Surrey SM1 3GH) and Christian Feminists (c/o Sheelagh Robinson, 22 Foreshore, Deptford, London SE8).

2. Janet Spedding, *Clergy Wives: A Sociology of Conformity*. Janet Spedding presented a lecture at the Women's Research and Resource Centre (190 Upper Street, London N1), the cassette transcription of which is available from the library.

3. Ibid.

4. A painfully pertinent example appeared in 1973, when a clergy wife initiated a lengthy correspondence in *The Times* over whether or not clergy wives should be included in *Crockford's Clerical Directory*. In 1976, during International Women's Year, Mrs Ruth Hook wrote a guest article for *The Times* entitled, 'How the Vicar's Wife makes Nonsense of Women's Lib' (4 February 1976). We draw on this article throughout this chapter as a rare serious treatment of the subject to appear in the national press over the last five years (see also n. 19).

5. Fuller details of various canonical enactments appear in F. L. Cross (ed.), *The Oxford Dictionary of the Christian Church*, Oxford University Press [2]1974, p. 259, s.v. 'Celibacy of the Clergy'. For an important discussion see now E. Schillebeeckx, *Ministry*, SCM Press 1981, pp. 85–99.

6. Augustine, *Of the Work of Monks*, translated by H. Browne, III, p. 524, quoted in Julia O'Faolain and Lauro Martines (eds.), *Not in God's Image: Women in History*, Virago 1979, p. 142.

7. Ibid., p. 194. From their survey of Erasmus, *Christiani matrimonii institutio* and *Colloquies*, the editors comment: 'The leading humanist of his day, Erasmus lent his authority to the still faint call for having girls pursue study, but he limited the ideal to the daughters of the rich and

nobly born. In the long run, however, education for highborn ladies was to be the thin end of the wedge.'

8. Germaine Greer, *The Female Eunuch*, Paladin 1971, p. 200.

9. Harington, *Brief View of the State of the Church* (1607).

10. James Nelson, *Embodiment*, SPCK 1980, concentrates largely on sexual questions and covers both patristic and Reformation theology.

11. Luther, *Table Talk* (1531), LIV, p. 171, quoted in *Not in God's Image*, p. 209.

12. *Table Talk*, LIV, p. 8, ibid.

13. John Calvin, *Institutes of the Christian Religion*, IV, xv, 21.

14. Rosemary Radford Ruether, *Mary, the Feminine Face of the Church*, SCM Press 1979, p. 5 (not in the US edition).

15. *Malleus Maleficarum* was published in 1486 by two Dominicans, Heinrich Kramer and Jacobus Sprenger. According to *Not in God's Image*, 'their catechism had gone through fourteen known editions' (by 1520). The *Malleus* itself, though singularly elusive when sought in historical and theological tomes (and mentioned only cursorily under 'Witchcraft' in *The Oxford Dictionary of the Christian Church*) is in print: translated by Montague Summers, Arrow Books 1971.

16. That is, a *Mr* Mary Wollstonecraft, a *Mr* George Eliot, a *Mr* Virginia Woolf.

17. *The Times*, 4 February 1976 (see n. 4 above).

18. It would be wearisome to recite the many instances of tabloid stereotypes of the vicar's wife. Suffice it to say that magazines and newspapers found Mrs Runcie's intention to continue teaching and playing the piano after her husband's elevation to the See of Canterbury worthy of comment!

19. Letter from Mrs Margaret Coombs, *Church Times*, February 1980.

20. Anthony Trollope, *Barchester Towers*, ch. 3.

21. Rosemary Radford Ruether, *Mary. The Feminine Face of the Church*, SCM Press 1979, p. 5.

22. An analysis and critique of housework, time spent, standards expected and male/female co-operation are an important theme of feminist discussion. See the comments by Betty Friedan quoted in ch. 1.

Chapter 7 Sisters of Cassandra

1. T. S. Eliot, 'Little Gidding', *Four Quartets*, Faber and Faber 1944 (the last line of Part III). Eliot echoes Mother Julian's imagery throughout the poem.

2. Dorothy L. Sayers, 'Are Women Human?', *Unpopular Opinions*, Gollancz 1947, p. 148.

3. Julian of Norwich, *Revelations of Divine Love*, Penguin Books 1966, p. 211.

4. Naomi Goldenberg, *The Changing of the Gods*, Beacon Press, Boston 1979, p. 22.

5. Women's study of language is a major explorative field – both secular

and theological. Studies mirror the general spectrum of feminist thought by ranging from a separatist to a restorative emphasis. Two examples here may be useful to the reader: 'Nowhere is women's experience of male-dominated language more pervasive than in the church and synagogue. Such "he" language is "applied in the generic sense" to God, to the preacher, to the worshipper. In hymns, liturgies and styles of government, religious life is male orientated. It is *generic nonsense* to say that women are included linguistically when they are excluded by so many practices. If this is to change, the Biblical, theological, and ecclesial traditions must be interpreted and translated so that the liberating power of God's love can break through in new words and actions. The search for a usable past includes the search for usable language and new forms of expression' (Letty Russell, *Human Liberation in a Feminist Perspective. A Theology*, Westminster Press, Philadelphia 1974, p. 95); 'Women have been systematically excluded from the English language; split off from the sounds, words, and syntax that should be our most powerful means of expressing our feeling, thoughts, and desires . . . Our separation from language defines and maintains our separation from our experience' (Julia Stanley, 'The Rhetoric of Denial: Delusion, Distortion, Deception', *Sinister Wisdom* 3, 1977, p. 28, quoted by Emily Culpepper, 'The Spiritual Movement of Radical Feminist Consciousness', in *Understanding the New Religions* (see ch. 1, note 1), p. 229).

6. Naomi Goldenberg, *The Changing of the Gods*, especially pp. 86–114.

7. Folklore and anecdote abound with observations about the brisk, sensible religion of the traditional Englishman, though the most oft-quoted must be the limerick about the young man of Moravia who did not need a saviour, and said:

'All a man needs
is to practise good deeds,
    for religion is decent behaviour' (anon).

8. Friends of the Earth, *The Stockholm Conference: Only One Earth*, Earth Island 1972, pp. 22–4.

9. Arthur Koestler, *Darkness at Noon*, Penguin Books 1947, p. 81 quoting from *De schismate libri* III, 1411.

10. Germaine Greer, *The Female Eunuch*, Paladin Books 1971, p. 317.

11. There was a rumour in circulation that a group at the *Pacem in Terris* conference in New York City had nominated the Bomb for the Nobel Peace Prize.

12. E. P. Thompson and Dan Smith (eds.), *Protest and Survive*, Penguin Books 1980, p. 45.

13. The musical *West Side Story* was a breakthrough into earthy raw realism in our youth (a welcome relief from a decade of unrelieved moonlight and roses!). But here too the women, sharp and unsentimental as they were, waited, dismissed with a flick of the finger, while the men held their war counsels and fights. The women colluded, when they themselves were used as pretexts for violence and unquestioningly gave comfort and shelter from victory or humiliation.

14. From Wilfred Owen's poem 'Parable of the Old Men and the Young', from *The Collected Poems of Wilfred Owen*, Chatto and Windus 1963. In this poem Owen comments on the failure of a professedly Christian civilization to give heed to God's prohibition of human sacrifice, revealed in the Old Testament story of Abraham and Isaac.

15. Adrienne Rich, *Of Woman Born*, Virago 1977, p. 269.

16. Secular progress, with the accompanying legal safeguards for women wanting to pursue careers around a young family, has been far-reaching in the last ten years. But women's traditionally specific needs in this area – nursery schools, crèches, etc. – are the first set of provisions to be threatened by economic cuts, usually accompanied with time-honoured public rationale about women's 'proper' responsibilities.

17. Arianna Stassinopolous, *The Female Woman*, David-Poynter 1973, p. 66.

18. Ibid., p. 132.

19. *The Poems of Alice Meynell*, Burns and Oates 1913, p. 86.

20. One example comes from Japan, where a liberal abortion law was rescinded in 1973 and the pill made unavailable when the falling birthrate began to threaten a cheap supply of labour. This practice has no political boundaries and cannot, as it often is, be associated exclusively with totalitarian left-wing regimes.

21. Arianna Stassinopolous, *The Female Woman*, p. 67.

22. Adrienne Rich, *Of Woman Born*, p. 279.

23. Eileen Egan,*Women and the Peace Message of Jesus*, a *Catholic Worker* Broadsheet, reprinted from the Catholic Worker, New York Fellowship Publications 1976.

24. A threat often allayed in Western culture, as Betty Friedan points out throughout *The Feminine Mystique*, by the intervention of psychiatry, designed to adjust the woman to her role; thus forbidding her on pain of being 'ill' to question whether her role is life-enhancing.

25. Dorothy Dinnerstein, *The Rocking of the Cradle and the Ruling of the World*, Harper and Row, New York 1976, p. 150.

Index